Learning to Follow Christ

365 Devos For Girls

Introduction

The decision to follow Jesus is the biggest, most important decision of your life. But once you've decided to follow Him, you still need daily reminders about God's rules, God's wisdom, and God's Son.

How do you start your day? Do you get yourself up early enough to spend a few quiet moments studying your Bible and thinking about the things that God wants you to know? Or are you one of those girls who sleeps until the last possible minute, leaving no time for matters of the heart and soul? Hopefully, you make a habit of spending time each morning with your Creator. When you do, you'll soon discover that God will help you make better decisions, decisions that will improve your own life and the lives of your friends and family.

This book contains 365 chapters, one for each day of the year. During the next 12 months, try this experiment: Read a chapter each day—and while you're at it, put at least one good idea into your head and your heart, at least one nugget of inspiration for the upcoming day. By giving God a few minutes each morning, you can change the direction of your thoughts and the quality of your choices.

Your daily devotional time can be habit-forming, and should be. The first few minutes of each day are invaluable—if you treat them that way and offer them to God, you'll never regret it.

The Decision to Follow Jesus

"Follow Me," Jesus told them, "and I will make you into fishers of men!" Immediately they left their nets and followed Him.

—Mark 1:17-18 Holman CSB

Your decision to follow Jesus is the most important decision of your life. Hopefully, you will follow Him today and every day from now on.

Jesus doesn't want you to be a run-of-the-mill, follow-the-crowd kind of girl. He wants you to be a "new creation" through Him. And that's exactly what you should want for yourself, too.

Jesus deserves your undivided attention and you deserve the experience of giving it to Him. So do yourself and your loved ones a favor: follow Christ today, and keep following Him. Your loved ones will be glad you did . . . and so will you.

Think of this—we may live together with Him here and now, a daily walking with Him who loved us and gave Himself for us.

Elisabeth Elliot

Spending Time with God

*Step out of the traffic! Take a long, loving look at me, your
High God, above politics, above everything*

—Psalm 46:10 MSG

Where does God fit into your day? Are you one of
those girls who tries to squeeze Him in on Sundays and at
mealtimes? Or do you talk to Him more often than that?

This book contains short devotional readings that you
can you in just a few minutes. So, if you read a chapter a
day for an entire year, you will have given God your undivided attention for at least a couple of minutes each day.
And make no mistake about it: the emphasis in the previ-
ous sentence should be placed on the words "at least."
In truth, you should give God lots more time than a few
minutes a day, but hey, it's a start.

Even if you're the busiest person on the planet, you
can still carve out a little time for God. And when you think
about it, isn't that the very least you should do?

God is a place of safety you can run to, but it helps if you
are running to Him on a daily basis so that you are in
familiar territory.

Stormie Omartian

Trusting the Quiet Voice

In quietness and trust is your strength.

—Isaiah 30:15 NASB

Whenever you're about to make an important decision, you should listen carefully to the quiet voice inside. Sometimes, of course, it's tempting to do otherwise. From time to time you'll be tempted to abandon your better judgment by ignoring your conscience. Don't do it!

Instead of ignoring that quiet little voice, pay careful attention to it. If you do, your conscience will lead you in the right direction—in fact, it's trying to lead you right now. So listen . . . and learn.

Arm yourself with the Word of God, and your conscience will sound off loud and clear when you're headed in the wrong direction.

Charles Stanley

God desires that we become spiritually healthy enough through faith to have a conscience that rightly interprets the work of the Holy Spirit.

Beth Moore

Eternal Life:
God's Priceless Gift

I have written these things to you who believe in the name of the Son of God, so that you may know that you have eternal life.

—1 John 5:13 Holman CSB

Christ sacrificed His life on the cross so that we might have eternal life. This gift, freely given from God's only begotten Son, is the priceless possession of everyone who accepts Him as Lord and Savior.

God is waiting patiently for each of us to accept the gift of eternal life. Let us claim Christ's gift today. Let us walk with the Savior, let us love Him, let us praise Him, and let us share His message with the world.

God offers you a priceless gift: the gift of eternal life. If you have not already done so, accept God's gift today—tomorrow may be too late.

The gift of God is eternal life, spiritual life, abundant life through faith in Jesus Christ, the Living Word of God.

Anne Graham Lotz

Christianity Here and Now

Teach me to do Your will, for You are my God. May Your gracious Spirit lead me on level ground.

—Psalm 143:10 Holman CSB

God doesn't want you to be a run-of-the-mill, follow-the-crowd kind of girl. God wants you to be a "new creation" through Him. And that's exactly what you should want for yourself, too.

Nothing is more important than your wholehearted commitment to your Creator and to His only begotten Son. Your faith must never be an afterthought; it must be your ultimate priority, your ultimate possession, and your ultimate passion.

You are the recipient of Christ's love. Accept it enthusiastically and share it passionately. Jesus deserves your extreme enthusiasm; the world deserves it; and you deserve the experience of sharing it.

How often it occurs to me, as it must to you, that it is far easier simply to cooperate with God!

Beth Moore

Expecting God's Blessings

My cup runs over. Surely goodness and mercy shall follow me all the days of my life; and I will dwell in the house of the Lord forever.

—Psalm 23:5-6 NKJV

Face facts: Christians have every reason to be optimistic and hopeful about life here on earth and life eternal. Mrs. Charles E. Cowman advised, "Never yield to gloomy anticipation. Place your hope and confidence in God. He has no record of failure."

Sometimes, despite our trust in God, we may fall into the spiritual traps of worry, frustration, anxiety, or sheer exhaustion, and our hearts become heavy. What's needed is plenty of rest, a large dose of perspective, and God's healing touch, but not necessarily in that order.

Today, make this promise to yourself and keep it: vow to be a hope-filled Christian. Think optimistically about your life, your education, your family, and your future. And then, when you've filled your heart with hope, share your optimism with others. They'll be better for it, and so will you.

It never hurts your eyesight to look on the bright side of things.

Barbara Johnson

Mistakes:
The Price of Being Human

LORD, help! they cried in their trouble, and he saved them from their distress.

—Psalm 107:13 NLT

Mistakes: nobody likes 'em but everybody makes 'em. Sometimes, even if you're a very good person, you're going to mess things up. And when you do, God is always ready to forgive you—He'll do His part, but you should be willing to do your part, too. Here's what you need to do:

1. If you've been engaging in behavior that is against the will of God, cease and desist (that means stop). 2. If you made a mistake, learn from it and don't repeat it (that's called getting smarter). 3. If you've hurt somebody, apologize and ask for forgiveness (that's called doing the right thing). 4. Ask for God's forgiveness, too (He'll give it whenever you ask, but you do need to ask!). Have you made a mistake? If so, today is the perfect day to make things right with everybody (and the word "everybody" includes yourself, your family, your friends, and your God).

Mistakes are the price you pay for being human; repeated mistakes are the price you pay for being stubborn. So don't be hardheaded: learn from your experiences—the first time!

Growing Up

When I was a child, I spoke and thought and reasoned as a child does. But when I grew up, I put away childish things.

—1 Corinthians 13:11 NLT

Growing up isn't easy, and it isn't speedy. The path to spiritual maturity unfolds day by day. Each day offers the opportunity to worship God, to ignore God, or to rebel against God. When we worship Him with our prayers, our words, our thoughts, and our actions, we are blessed by the richness of our relationship with the Father. But if we ignore God altogether or intentionally rebel against His commandments, we rob ourselves of His blessings.

Today offers yet another opportunity for spiritual growth. If you choose, you can seize that opportunity by obeying God's Word, by seeking His will, and by walking with His Son.

God will help us become the people we are meant to be, if only we will ask Him.

Hannah Whitall Smith

Beyond Stubbornness

Pride comes before destruction, and an arrogant spirit before a fall.

—Proverbs 16:18 Holman CSB

Since the days of Adam and Eve, human beings have been strong-willed and rebellious. Our rebellion stems, in large part, from an intense desire to do things "our way" instead of "God's way." But when we pridefully choose to forsake God's path for our lives, we do ourselves a sincere injustice . . . and we are penalized because of our stubbornness.

God's Word warns us to be humble, not prideful. God instructs us to be obedient, not rebellious. God wants us to do things His way. When we do, we earn lots of blessings—more blessings than we can count. But when we pridefully rebel against our Creator, we sow the seeds of our own problems and we reap a sad, sparse, bitter harvest. May we sow—and reap—accordingly.

Much bending breaks the bough; much unbending the mind.

Francis Bacon

Real Faith

For in it God's righteousness is revealed from faith to faith, just as it is written: The righteous will live by faith.

—Romans 1:17 Holman CSB

Jesus wants to have a real relationship with you. Are you willing to have a real relationship with Him? Unless you can answer this question with a resounding "Yes," you may miss out on some wonderful things.

This day offers yet another opportunity to behave yourself like a real Christian. And it's yet another chance to put God first in your life. When you do, God will guide your steps and bless your endeavors . . . forever.

The Christian life is one of faith, where we find ourselves routinely overdriving our headlights but knowing it's okay because God is in control and has a purpose behind it.

Bill Hybels

Faith in God is a terrific venture in the dark.

Oswald Chambers

Faith is a strong power, mastering any difficulty in the strength of the Lord who made heaven and earth.

Corrie ten Boom

Choices That Make
a Difference

The thing you should want most is God's kingdom and doing what God wants. Then all these other things you need will be given to you.

—Matthew 6:33 NCV

There's really no way to get around it: choices matter. If you make good choices, good things will usually happen to you. And if you make bad choices, bad things will usually happen.

The next time you have an important choice to make, ask yourself this: "Am I doing what God wants me to do?" If you can answer that question with a great big "YES," then go ahead. But if you're not sure if the choice you are about to make is right, slow down. Why? Because choices matter . . . a lot!

Choices can change our lives profoundly. The choice to mend a broken relationship, to say "yes" to a difficult assignment, to lay aside some important work to play with a child, to visit some forgotten person—these small choices may affect many lives eternally.

Gloria Gaither

Directing Our Thoughts

Finally brothers, whatever is true, whatever is honorable, whatever is just, whatever is pure, whatever is lovely, whatever is commendable—if there is any moral excellence and if there is any praise—dwell on these things.

—Philippians 4:8 Holman CSB

Okay girlfriend, here's a question: How will you direct your thoughts today? Will you obey the words of Philippians 4:8 by dwelling upon those things that are honorable, pure, and worthy of praise? Or will you allow your thoughts to be hijacked by the negativity that seems to dominate our troubled world?

Are you fearful, angry, bored, or worried? Are you so preoccupied with the concerns of this day that you fail to thank God for the promise of eternity? Are you confused or pessimistic? If so, God wants to have a little talk with you. He wants to remind you of His infinite love and His boundless grace. As you contemplate these things, and as you give thanks for God's blessings, negativity should no longer dominate your day or your life.

Preoccupy my thoughts with your praise beginning today.

Joni Eareckson Tada

Answered Prayers

God answered their prayers because they trusted him.

—1 Chronicles 5:20 MSG

God answers our prayers. What God does not do is this: He does not answer our prayers in a time and fashion of our choosing, and He does not always answer our prayers by saying, "Yes." Sometimes our loving Heavenly Father responds to our requests by saying "No," and we must accept His answer, even though we may not understand it.

God answers prayers not according to our wishes but according to His master plan. We cannot know that plan, but we can know the Planner . . . and we must trust His wisdom, His righteousness, and His unending love.

What God gives in answer to our prayers will always be the thing we most urgently need, and it will always be sufficient.

Elisabeth Elliot

Know When to Say No

Wisdom will save you from the ways of wicked men....

—Proverbs 2:12 NIV

It happens to all of us at one time or another: a friend asks us to do something that we think is wrong. What should we do? Should we try to please our friend by doing something bad? No way! It's not worth it!

Trying to please our friends is okay. What's not okay is misbehaving in order to do so. Do you have a friend who encourages you to misbehave? Hopefully you don't have any friends like that. But if you do, say, "No, NO, NOOOOOO!" And what if your friend threatens to break up the friendship? Let her! Friendships like that just aren't worth it.

You will get untold flak for prioritizing God's revealed and present will for your life over man's . . . but, boy, is it worth it.

Beth Moore

Give God what's right—not what's left!

Anonymous

It's Not Hard to Be Kind

Therefore, God's chosen ones, holy and loved, put on heartfelt compassion, kindness, humility, gentleness, and patience.

—Colossians 3:12 Holman CSB

How hard is it to say a kind word? Not very! Yet sometimes we're so busy that we forget to say the very things that might make other people feel better.

We should always try to say nice things to our families and friends. And when we feel like saying something that's not so nice, perhaps we should stop and think before we say it. Kind words help; cruel words hurt. It's as simple as that. And, when we say the right thing at the right time, we give a gift that can change someone's day or someone's life.

When we do little acts of kindness that make life more bearable for someone else, we are walking in love as the Bible commands us.

Barbara Johnson

Do all the good you can. By all the means you can. In all the ways you can. In all the places you can. At all the times you can. To all the people you can. As long as you can.

John Wesley

Making Better Decisions

Don't turn your back on wisdom, for she will protect you. Love her, and she will guard you.

—Proverbs 4:6 NLT

Decisions—you've already made millions of them, and you've still got millions more to make. Most of these choices are of the smaller variety—like what to do at a given moment, or what to say, or what to wear, or how to direct your thoughts. But a few of your decisions will be BIG, like choosing to be a Christian, or deciding whether or not to stay in school, or choosing a profession. Whatever choices you face—whether they're big, little, or somewhere in between—you can be sure that the quality of those choices will make a huge difference in the quality of your life.

How can you make better decisions? A great place to start is by talking things over with God before you spring into action, not after. While you're at it, you can check things out with your parents—or with other concerned adults, like grandparents or teachers. And, you can learn to listen carefully to your conscience.

During the coming year, as you think about the lessons in this book, please take these ideas seriously. When you do, you'll make decisions that will please God and improve your life.

Beyond Anger

Mockers can get a whole town agitated, but those who are wise will calm anger.

—Proverbs 29:8 NLT

Are you sometimes a hotheaded girl? If so, here's something to remember: Your temper is either your master or your servant. Either you control it, or it controls you. And the extent to which you allow anger to rule your life will determine, to a surprising extent, the quality of your relationships with others and your relationship with God.

Anger and peace cannot coexist in the same mind. So obey God's Word by turning away from anger today and every day. You'll be glad you did, and so will your family and friends.

Life is too short to spend it being angry, bored, or dull.

Barbara Johnson

Anger is the noise of the soul; the unseen irritant of the heart; the relentless invader of silence.

Max Lucado

Order your soul;
reduce your wants;
associate in Christian community;
obey the laws;
trust in Providence.

—

St. Augustine

The Possessions We Own, and Vice Versa

We brought nothing into the world, so we can take nothing out. But, if we have food and clothes, we will be satisfied with that.

—1 Timothy 6:7-8 NCV

How important is the stuff you own? Not as important as you might think. In the life of a committed Christian, material possessions should play a rather small role. In fact, when we become overly enamored with the things we own, we needlessly distance ourselves from the peace that God offers to those who place Him at the center of their lives.

Of course, we all need the basic necessities of life, but once we meet those needs for ourselves and for our families, the piling up of possessions creates more problems than it solves. Our real riches, of course, are not of this world. We are never really rich until we are rich in spirit.

Are you one of those girls who sometimes finds herself wrapped up in the concerns of the material world? If so, it's time to reorder your priorities by turning your thoughts and your prayers to more important matters. And, it's time to begin storing up riches that will endure throughout eternity: the spiritual kind.

The Plan According to God

I will instruct you and show you the way to go; with My eye on you, I will give counsel.

—Psalm 32:8 Holman CSB

Maybe you've heard this old saying: "Look before you leap." Well, that saying may be old, but it still applies to you. Before you jump into something, you should look ahead and plan ahead. Otherwise, you might soon be sorry you jumped!

When you acquire the habit of planning ahead, you'll usually make better choices. So when it comes to the important things in life, make a plan and stick to it. When you do, you'll think about the consequences of your actions before you do something silly . . . or dangerous . . . or both.

It's incredible to realize that what we do each day has meaning in the big picture of God's plan.

Bill Hybels

You can't start building a better tomorrow if you wait till tomorrow to start building.

Marie T. Freeman

For God So Loved the World

This is how much God loved the world: He gave his Son, his one and only Son. And this is why: so that no one need be destroyed; by believing in him anyone can have a whole and lasting life.

—John 3:16 MSG

For Christians, death is not an ending; it is a beginning; for believers, the grave is not a final resting-place, it is a place of transition. For Christians, death is not a dark journey into nothingness; it is a homecoming.

God sent His Son as a sacrifice for our sins. Through Jesus, we are redeemed. By welcoming Christ into our hearts, we have received the precious, unfathomable gift of eternal life. Let us praise God for His Son. The One from Galilee has saved us from our sins so that we might live courageously, die triumphantly, and live again—eternally.

If you are a believer, your judgment will not determine your eternal destiny. Christ's finished work on Calvary was applied to you the moment you accepted Christ as Savior.

Beth Moore

Celebrating God's Handiwork

Christ is the visible image of the invisible God. He existed before God made anything at all and is supreme over all creation.

—Colossians 1:15 NLT

When we consider God's glorious universe, we marvel at the miracle of nature. The smallest seedlings and grandest stars are all part of God's infinite creation. God has placed His handiwork on display for all to see, and if we are wise, we will make time each day to celebrate the world that surrounds us.

Today, pause to consider the majesty of heaven and earth. It is as miraculous as it is beautiful, as incomprehensible as it is breathtaking.

The Psalmist reminds us that the heavens are a declaration of God's glory. May we never cease to praise the Father for a universe that stands as an awesome testimony to His presence and His power.

God writes the gospel not in the Bible alone, but on the trees, and flowers, and clouds, and stars.

Martin Luther

Today Is Your Classroom

If you teach the wise, they will get knowledge.

—Proverbs 21:11 NCV

Today is your classroom: what will you learn? Will you use today's experiences as tools for personal growth, or will you ignore the lessons that life and God are trying to teach you? Will you carefully study God's Word, and will you apply His teachings to the experiences of everyday life? The events of today have much to teach. You have much to learn. May you live—and learn—accordingly.

Salvation is the process that's done, that's secure, that no one can take away from you. Sanctification is the lifelong process of being changed from one degree of glory to the next, growing in Christ, putting away the old, taking on the new.

Max Lucado

True learning can take place at every age of life, and it doesn't have to be in the curriculum plan.

Suzanne Dale Ezell

Share Your Blessings

Remember this: the person who sows sparingly will also reap sparingly, and the person who sows generously will also reap generously.

—2 Corinthians 9:6 Holman CSB

Here's a fact that every girl (including you) should know: it pays to be generous.

Jesus told us that we should be generous with other people, but sometimes we don't feel much like sharing. Instead of sharing the things that we have, we want to keep them all to ourselves. But God doesn't want selfishness to rule our hearts; He wants us to be generous.

Are you lucky enough to have nice stuff? If so, God's instructions are clear: you must share your blessings with others. And that's exactly the way it should be. After all, think how generous God has been with you.

We can't do everything, but can we do anything more valuable than invest ourselves in another?

Elisabeth Elliot

Scattering Seeds of Kindness

Be devoted to one another in brotherly love. Honor one another above yourselves.

—Romans 12:10 NIV

How do you define the word "friend"? The dictionary defines it as "a person who is attached to another by feelings of affection or personal regard." This definition is accurate, as far as it goes, but when we examine the deeper meaning of friendship, so many more descriptors come to mind: trustworthiness, loyalty, helpfulness, kindness, understanding, forgiveness, encouragement, humor, and cheerfulness, to mention but a few.

How wonderful are the joys of friendship. Today, as you consider the many blessings that God has given you, remember to thank Him for the friends He has chosen to place along your path. May you be a blessing to them, and may they richly bless you today, tomorrow, and every day that you live.

A person who really cares about his or her neighbor, a person who genuinely loves others, is a person who bears witness to the truth.

Anne Graham Lotz

Make Today a Day of Celebration

Always be full of joy in the Lord. I say it again—rejoice!

—Philippians 4:4 NLT

What is the best day to celebrate life? This one! Today and every day should be a time for celebration as we consider all the things that God has done.

What do you expect from the day ahead? Are you expecting God to do wonderful things, or are you living beneath a cloud of worry and doubt?

The familiar words of Psalm 118:24 remind us of a profound yet simple truth: "This is the day which the LORD has made." Our duty, as believers, is to rejoice in God's marvelous creation. For Christians, every day begins and ends with God and His Son. Christ came to this earth to give us abundant life and eternal salvation. We give thanks to our Maker when we treasure each day. So with no further delay, let the celebration begin!

The highest and most desirable state of the soul is to praise God in celebration for being alive.

Luci Swindoll

Getting God's Wisdom

Understanding is like a fountain which gives life to those who use it.

—Proverbs 16:22 NCV

Wisdom is like a savings account: If you add to it consistently, then eventually you will have accumulated a great sum. The secret to success is consistency.

Whether you're twelve or a hundred and twelve, you've still got lots to learn. Even if you're a wise person, God isn't finished with you yet. Lifetime learning is part of God's plan, and He certainly hasn't finished teaching you some very important lessons.

The ultimate source of wisdom, of course, is the Word of God. When you study God's Word and live according to His commandments, you will accumulate wisdom day by day. And finally, with God's help, you'll have enough wisdom to keep and enough left over to share.

Most of us go through life praying a little, planning a little, jockeying for position, hoping but never being quite certain of anything, and always secretly afraid that we will miss the way. This is a tragic waste of truth and never gives rest to the heart. There is a better way. It is to repudiate our own wisdom and take instead the infinite wisdom of God.

A. W. Tozer

White Lies?

Doing what is right brings freedom to honest people.

—Proverbs 11:6 ICB

Sometimes, people convince themselves that it's okay to tell "little white lies." Sometimes people convince themselves that itsy bitsy lies aren't harmful. But there's a problem: little lies have a way of growing into big ones, and once they grow up, they cause lots of problems.

Remember that lies, no matter what size, are not part of God's plan for our lives, so tell the truth about everything. It's the right thing to do, and besides: when you always tell the truth, you don't have to try and remember what you said!

Those who are given to white lies soon become color blind.

Anonymous

A lie is like a snowball: the further you roll it, the bigger it becomes.

Martin Luther

Much guilt arises in the life of the believer from practicing the chameleon life of environmental adaptation.

Beth Moore

Difficult Days

We take the good days from God—why not also the bad days?

—Job 2:10 MSG

Face it: some days are better than others. But even on the days when you don't feel very good, God never leaves you for even a moment. So if you need assistance, you can always pray to God, knowing that He will listen and help.

If you're feeling unhappy, talk things over with God, and while you're at it, be sure and talk things over with your parents, too. And remember this: the sooner you start talking, the sooner things will get better.

When life is difficult, God wants us to have a faith that trusts and waits.

Kay Arthur

Our heavenly Father never takes anything from his children unless he means to give them something better.

George Mueller

Let God's promises shine on your problems.

Corrie ten Boom

Your To-Do List . . . and God's

Come near to God, and God will come near to you. You sinners, clean sin out of your lives. You who are trying to follow God and the world at the same time, make your thinking pure.

—James 4:8 NCV

When you make God's priorities your priorities, you will receive God's blessings. When you make God a full partner in every aspect of your life, He will lead you along the proper path: His path. When you allow God to reign over your heart, He will honor you with spiritual blessings that are simply too numerous to count. So, as you plan for the day ahead, make God's will your ultimate priority. When you do, every other priority will have a tendency to fall neatly into place.

With God, it's never "Plan B" or "second best." It's always "Plan A." And, if we let Him, He'll make something beautiful of our lives.

Gloria Gaither

God Solves Problems

Since God assured us, "I'll never let you down, never walk off and leave you," we can boldly quote, God is there, ready to help; I'm fearless no matter what. Who or what can get to me?

—Hebrews 13:5-6 MSG

Do you have a problem that you haven't been able to solve? Welcome to the club! Life is full of problems that don't have easy solutions. But if you have a problem that you can't solve, there is something you can do: turn that problem over to God. He can handle it.

God has a way of solving our problems if we let Him; our job is to let Him. God can handle things that we can't. And the sooner we turn our concerns over to Him, the sooner He will go to work solving those troubles that are simply too big for us to handle.

If you're worried or discouraged, pray about it. And ask your parents and friends to pray about it, too. And then stop worrying because no problem is too big for God; not even yours.

God is always sufficient in perfect proportion to our need.

Beth Moore

Learn from Ants

Go to the ant, O sluggard. Observe her ways and be wise: which, having no chief, officer or ruler, prepares her food in the summer and gathers her provision in the harvest. How long will you lie down, O sluggard? When will you arise from your sleep?

—Proverbs 6:6-9 NASB

The Bible instructs us that we can learn an important lesson from a surprising source: ants. Ants are among nature's most industrious creatures. They do their work without supervision and without hesitation. We should do likewise.

God's Word is clear: We are instructed to work diligently and faithfully. We are told that the fields are ripe for the harvest, that the workers are few, and that the importance of our work is profound. Let us work hard for our Master without hesitation and without complaint. Nighttime is coming. Until it does, let us honor our Heavenly Father with grateful hearts and willing hands.

Wouldn't it make an astounding difference, not only in the quality of the work we do, but also in the satisfaction, even our joy, if we recognized God's gracious gift in every single task?

Elisabeth Elliot

His Love Lasts Forever

I am the good shepherd. The good shepherd lays down his life for the sheep.

—John 10:11 Holman CSB

You probably can't remember the first time you heard the song "Jesus Loves Me." It's a happy little song that should remind you of a very important fact: Jesus loves you very much.

When you invite Jesus into your heart, He will be your friend forever. If you make mistakes, He'll still be your friend. When you aren't perfect, He'll still love you. If you feel sorry or sad, He can help you feel better.

Yes, Jesus loves you . . . and you should love yourself. So the next time you're feeling blue about yourself . . . or something that you've done . . . remember that Jesus loves you, your family loves you, and you should feel that way, too.

Live your lives in love, the same sort of love which Christ gives us, and which He perfectly expressed when He gave Himself as a sacrifice to God.

Corrie ten Boom

Spiritual Wealth

Trust in your money and down you go! But the godly flourish like leaves in spring.

—Proverbs 11:28 NLT

Sometimes it's hard being a Christian, especially when the world keeps pumping out messages that are contrary to your faith.

The media is working around the clock in an attempt to rearrange your priorities. The media says that your appearance is all-important, that your clothes are all-important, that your relationships with the opposite sex are all-important, and that partying is all-important. But guess what? Those messages are lies. The "all-important" things in your life have little to do with parties and appearances. The all-important things in life have to do with your faith, your family, and your future. Period.

Are you a girl who's willing to stand up for her faith? Are you willing to stand up and be counted, not just in church, where it's relatively easy to be a Christian, but also out there in the "real" world, where it's hard? Hopefully so, because you owe it to God and you owe it to yourself.

He who dies with the most toys . . . still dies.

Anonymous

Laughing with Life

A happy heart makes the face cheerful, but heartache crushes the spirit.

—Proverbs 15:13 NIV

Laughter is medicine for the soul, but sometimes, we forget to take our medicine. And that's too bad.

The next time you find yourself dwelling on the negatives of life, refocus your attention to things positive. The next time you're feeling down, stop yourself and turn your thoughts around. And, if you see your glass as "half empty," you can be sure that your spiritual vision is impaired. With God, your glass is never half empty. With God, your glass is filled to the brim and overflowing . . . forever.

Today, as you go about your daily activities, approach life with a smile on your lips and hope in your heart. And laugh every chance you get. After all, God created laughter for a reason...and Father indeed knows best. So laugh!

When we bring sunshine into the lives of others, we're warmed by it ourselves. When we spill a little happiness, it splashes on us.

Barbara Johnson

Your One-of-a-Kind Family

Love must be without hypocrisy. Detest evil; cling to what is good. Show family affection to one another with brotherly love. Outdo one another in showing honor.

—Romans 12:9–10 Holman CSB

Your family is a wonderful, one-of-a-kind gift from God. And your family members love you very much—what a blessing it is to be loved!

Have you ever really stopped to think about how much you are loved? Your parents love you (of course) and so does everybody else in your family. But it doesn't stop there. You're also an important part of God's family . . . and He loves you more than you can imagine.

What should you do about all the love that comes your way? You should accept it; you should be thankful for it; and you should share it . . . starting now!

I like to think of my family as a big, beautiful patchwork quilt—each of us so different yet stitched together by love and life experiences.

Barbara Johnson

A home is a place where we find direction.

Gigi Graham Tchividjian

Love That Lasts

It is good and pleasant when God's people live together in peace!

—Psalm 133:1 NCV

As you know by now, the world is filled with people: some kind, and some not so kind. So here's a simple question: Are your friends kind to you? And are your friends nice to other people, too? If so, congratulations! If not, it's probably time to start looking for a few new friends. After all, it's really not very much fun to be around people who aren't nice to everybody.

The Bible teaches that a pure heart is a wonderful blessing. It's up to each of us to fill our hearts with love for God, love for Jesus, and love for all people. When we do, we feel better about ourselves.

Do you want to be the best person you can be? Then invite the love of Christ into your heart and share His love with your family and friends. And remember that lasting love always comes from a pure heart . . . like yours!

Inasmuch as anyone pushes you nearer to God, he or she is your friend.

Barbara Johnson

Whatever It Is,
God Is Bigger

Jesus turned around and said to her, "Daughter, be encouraged! Your faith has made you well." And the woman was healed at that moment.

—Matthew 9:22 NLT

How can you strengthen your faith? Through praise, through worship, through Bible study, and through prayer. And, as your faith becomes stronger, you will find ways to share it with your friends, your family, and with the world. When you place your faith, your trust, indeed your life in the hands of Christ Jesus, you'll be amazed at the marvelous things He can do with you and through you; so trust God's plans. With Him, all things are possible, and whatever "it" is, God is bigger.

No giant will ever be a match for a big God with a little rock.

Beth Moore

Following God will require faith and action. Without faith you will not be able to please God. When you act in faith, God is pleased.

Henry Blackaby and Claude King

Finding Comfort

I was very worried, but you comforted me . . . .

—Psalm 94:19 NCV

It is simply a fact of life: sometimes, you worry. Maybe you worry about the little stuff or maybe you worry about big stuff, but in either case, your mind wanders into bad spots. So where is the best place to take your worries? Take them to God. Take your troubles to Him; take your fears to Him; take your doubts to Him; take your weaknesses to Him; take your sorrows to Him . . . and leave them all there. Seek protection from the One who offers you eternal life; build your spiritual house upon the Rock that cannot be moved.

Give your cares to Him who cares for the flowers of the field. Rest assured He will also care for you.

C. H. Spurgeon

Worry is the senseless process of cluttering up tomorrow's opportunities with leftover problems from today.

Barbara Johnson

God Cares

For the Lord your God is the God of gods and Lord of lords, the great, mighty, and awesome God.

—Deuteronomy 10:17 Holman CSB

It's a promise that is made over and over again in the Bible: Whatever "it" is, God can handle it.

Life isn't always easy. Far from it! Sometimes, life can be very, very tough. But even then, even during our darkest moments, we're protected by a loving Heavenly Father. When we're worried, God can reassure us; when we're sad, God can comfort us. When our hearts are broken, God is not just near; He is here. So we must lift our thoughts and prayers to Him. When we do, He will answer our prayers. Why? Because He is our Shepherd, and He has promised to protect us now and forever.

The next time you're disappointed, don't panic. Don't give up. Just be patient and let God remind you he's still in control.

Max Lucado

Measure the size of the obstacles against the size of God.

Beth Moore

The Wisdom of Kindness

Kind people do themselves a favor, but cruel people bring trouble on themselves.

—Proverbs 11:17 NCV

If we believe the words of Proverbs 11:17—and we should—then we understand that kindness is its own reward. And, if we are to obey the commandments of our Savior—and we should—we must sow seeds of kindness wherever we go.

Kindness, compassion, and forgiveness are hallmarks of our Christian faith. So today, in honor of the One who first showed compassion for us, let's teach our families and friends the art of kindness through our words and through our deeds. Our loved ones are watching…and so is God.

If we have the true love of God in our hearts, we will show it in our lives. We will not have to go up and down the earth proclaiming it. We will show it in everything we say or do.

D. L. Moody

The attitude of kindness is everyday stuff like a great pair of sneakers. Not frilly. Not fancy. Just plain and comfortable.

Barbara Johnson

Obedience and Praise

Praise the Lord! Happy are those who respect the Lord, who want what he commands.

—Psalm 112:1 NCV

Psalm 112 links two powerful principles: obedience and praise. One of the most important ways that we can praise God is by obeying Him. As believers who have been saved by a risen Christ, we must worship our Creator, not only with our prayers and our words, but also with our actions.

Are you grateful for God's glorious gifts? Are you thankful for the treasure of eternal life that is yours through the sacrifice of God's Son Jesus? Of course you are. And one of the very best ways to express your gratitude to God is through obedience to the unchanging commandments of His Holy Word.

Holiness has never been the driving force of the majority. It is, however, mandatory for anyone who wants to enter the kingdom.

Elisabeth Elliot

New Life

When we were baptized, we were buried with Christ and shared his death. So, just as Christ was raised from the dead by the wonderful power of the Father, we also can live a new life.

—Romans 6:4 NCV

For faithful Christians, every day begins and ends with God and with His Son. Christ came to this earth to give us abundant life and eternal life. Our task is to accept Christ's grace with joy in our hearts as we receive the "new life" that can be ours through Him.

Believers who fashion their days around Jesus are transformed: They see the world differently; they act differently, and they feel differently about themselves and their neighbors.

Thoughtful Christians face the inevitable challenges and disappointments of each day armed with the joy of Christ and the promise of salvation. So whatever this day holds for you, begin it and end it with God as your partner and Christ as your Savior. And throughout the day, give thanks to the One who created you and saved you. God's love for you is infinite. Accept it joyously and be thankful.

We can be victorious, but only if we walk with God.

Beth Moore

Sharing Your Stuff

And God will generously provide all you need. Then you will always have everything you need and plenty left over to share with others.

—2 Corinthians 9:8 NLT

Are you one of those girls who is lucky enough to have a closet full of stuff? If so, it's probably time to share some of it.

When it's time to clean up your closet and give some things away, don't be upset. Instead of complaining, think about all the people who could enjoy the things that you don't use very much. And while you're at it, think about what Jesus might tell you to do if He were here. Jesus would tell you to share generously and cheerfully. And that's exactly what you should do!

The more we stuff ourselves with material pleasures, the less we seem to appreciate life.

Barbara Johnson

Your Amazing Talents!

Now there are different gifts, but the same Spirit. There are different ministries, but the same Lord.

—1 Corinthians 12:4-5 Holman CSB

Face facts: you're a girl with very special talents, talents that have been given to you by God. So here's a question: will you use your talents or not? God wants you to use your talents to become a better person and a better Christian. And that's what you should want for yourself.

As you're trying to figure out exactly what you're good at, be sure and talk about it with your parents. They can help you decide how best to use and improve the gifts God has given you.

In the great orchestra we call life, you have an instrument and a song, and you owe it to God to play them both sublimely.

Max Lucado

Natural abilities are like natural plants; they need pruning by study.

Francis Bacon

The Power of Hope

I wait quietly before God, for my hope is in him.

—Psalm 62:5 NLT

The self-fulfilling prophecy is alive, well, and living at your house. If you trust God and have faith for the future, your optimistic beliefs will give you direction and motivation. That's one reason that you should never lose hope, but certainly not the only reason. The primary reason that you, as a believer, should never lose hope, is because of God's unfailing promises.

Make no mistake about it: thoughts are powerful things. Your thoughts have the power to lift you up or to hold you down. When you acquire the habit of hopeful thinking, you will have acquired a powerful tool for improving your life. So if you find yourself falling into the spiritual traps of worry and discouragement, seek the healing touch of Jesus and the encouraging words of fellow Christians. And if you fall into the terrible habit of negative thinking, think again. After all, God's Word teaches us that Christ can overcome every difficulty (John 16:33). And when God makes a promise, He keeps it.

What we believe determines how we behave, and both determine what we become.

Warren Wiersbe

God Is Faithful

I have set the Lord always before me; because He is at my right hand I shall not be moved.

—Psalm 16:8 NKJV

God is faithful. He keeps His promises to us even when we stray far from His will. He continues to love us even when we disobey His commandments. But God does not force His blessings upon us. If we are to experience His love and His grace, we must claim them for ourselves.

Are you discouraged or fearful? Be comforted: God is with you. Are you confused? Listen to the quiet voice of your Heavenly Father. Are you angry? Talk with God and seek His guidance. Are you celebrating a great victory? Thank God and praise Him. He is the Giver of all things good.

In whatever condition you find yourself, wherever you are, whether you are happy or sad, victorious or vanquished, troubled or triumphant, remember that God is faithful and that His love is eternal. And be comforted. God is not just near. He is here.

If God chooses to remain silent, faith is content.

Ruth Bell Graham

A Fruitful Friendship

I am the Vine, you are the branches. When you're joined with me and I with you, the relation intimate and organic, the harvest is sure to be abundant.

—John 15:5 MSG

Whether you realize it or not, you already have a relationship with Jesus. Hopefully, it's a close relationship! Why? Because the friendship you form with Jesus will help you every day of your life . . . and beyond!

You can either be a girl who invites Jesus into your heart, or you can ignore Him altogether. Welcome Him today—and while you're at it, encourage your friends and family members to do the same.

Jesus—the standard of measurement, the scale of weights, the test of character for the whole moral universe.

R. G. Lee

In your greatest weakness, turn to your greatest strength, Jesus, and hear Him say, "My grace is sufficient for you, for My strength is made perfect in weakness" (2 Corinthians 12:9, NKJV).

Lisa Whelchel

Forgiveness Is Essential

The discretion of a man makes him slow to anger, and his glory is to overlook a transgression.

—Proverbs 19:11 NCV

Bitterness is a form of self-punishment; forgiveness is a means of self-liberation. Bitterness focuses on the injustices of the past; forgiveness focuses on the blessings of the present and the opportunities of the future. Bitterness is an emotion that hurts you; forgiveness is a decision that empowers you. Bitterness is foolishness; forgiveness is wisdom.

When we make God's priorities our priorities, He will lead us according to His plan and according to His commandments. When we study God's Word, we are reminded that God's reality is the ultimate reality. May we live—and forgive—accordingly.

If Jesus forgave those who nailed Him to the Cross, and if God forgives you and me, how can you withhold your forgiveness from someone else?

Anne Graham Lotz

Whom Should You Please?

A tranquil heart is life to the body, but jealousy is rottenness to the bones.

—Proverbs 14:30 Holman CSB

Sometimes, it's very tempting to be a people-pleaser. But usually, it's the wrong thing to do.

When you worry too much about pleasing dates or friends, you may not worry enough about pleasing God— and when you fail to please God, you inevitably pay a very high price for your mistaken priorities.

Whom will you try to please today: God or your friends? Your obligation is most certainly not to your peers or to your date. Your obligation is to an all-knowing and perfect God. Trust Him always. Love Him always. Praise Him always. And seek to please Him and only Him. Always.

We, as God's people, are not only to stay far away from sin and sinners who would entice us, but we are to be so like our God that we mourn over sin.

Kay Arthur

Those who follow the crowd usually get lost in it.

Rick Warren

Do you want to be wise?
Choose wise friends.

—

Charles Swindoll

Amazing Grace

Saving is all [God's] idea, and all his work. All we do is trust him enough to let him do it. It's God's idea from start to finish! We don't play the major role. If we did, we'd probably go around bragging that we'd done the whole thing! No, we neither make nor save ourselves. God does both the making and the saving.

—Ephesians 2:8-9 MSG

Here's the great news: God's grace is not earned . . . and thank goodness it's not! If God's grace were some sort of reward for good behavior, none of us could earn enough brownie points to win the big prize. But it doesn't work that way. Grace is a free offer from God. By accepting that offer, we transform our lives today and forever.

God's grace is not just any old gift; it's the ultimate gift, and we owe Him our eternal gratitude. Our Heavenly Father is waiting patiently for each of us to accept His Son and receive His grace. Let us accept that gift today so that we might enjoy God's presence now and throughout all eternity.

It is because of God's loving grace that Jesus died on the cross for our sins so we could experience an eternal relationship with Him.

Bill Bright

Encourage Each Other

So encourage each other and give each other strength, just as you are doing now.

—1 Thessalonians 5:11 NCV

Your optimism is contagious; feel free to share it with your friends. Your pessimism, too, is contagious; please keep it to yourself. After all, our world already has a lifetime supply of pessimism, cynicism, negativity, and doubt. Your voice should not be added to that chorus.

In Ephesians, Paul advises, "Do not let any unwholesome talk come out of your mouths, but only what is helpful for building others up according to their needs, that it may benefit those who listen" (4:29 NIV). Paul's words still apply. Most of your friends and family members need more encouragement and less criticism. So be a booster, not a cynic; your friends will be better for it, and so will you. But not necessarily in that order.

One of the ways God refills us after failure is through the blessing of Christian fellowship. Just experiencing the joy of simple activities shared with other children of God can have a healing effect on us.

Anne Graham Lotz

Looking for the Good

Dear friend, do not imitate what is evil, but what is good. The one who does good is of God; the one who does evil has not seen God.

—3 John 1:11 Holman CSB

If you look for the good in other people, you'll probably find it. And, if you look for the good things in life, you'll probably find them, too.

But if spend your time looking for things that aren't so good, you'll most certainly find plenty of bad things to look at. So what should you do? It's simple: you should look for the good things, of course.

When you start looking for good things, you'll find them everywhere: in church, at school, in your neighborhood, and at home.

So don't waste your time on things that make you feel angry, discouraged, worried, guilty, or afraid. Look, instead, for the good things in life, the things that God wants you to pay attention to. You'll be glad you did . . . and God will be glad, too.

The Golden Rule starts at home, but it should never stop there.

Marie T. Freeman

Cheerful Christianity

A joyful heart is good medicine, but a broken spirit dries up the bones.

—Proverbs 17:22 Holman CSB

Few things in life are more sad, or, for that matter, more absurd, than a grumpy Christian. Christ promises us lives of abundance and joy, but He does not force His joy upon us. We must claim His joy for ourselves, and when we do, Jesus, in turn, fills our spirits with His power and His love.

How can we receive from Christ the joy that is rightfully ours? By giving Him what is rightfully His: our hearts and our souls.

When we earnestly commit ourselves to the Savior of mankind, when we place Jesus at the center of our lives and trust Him as our personal Savior, He will transform us, not just for today, but for all eternity. Then we, as God's children, can share Christ's joy and His message with a world that needs both.

We may run, walk, stumble, drive, or fly, but let us never lose sight of the reason for the journey, or miss a chance to see a rainbow on the way.

Gloria Gaither

Remembering God's Love

For the Lord is good, and His love is eternal; His faithfulness endures through all generations.

—Psalm 100:5 Holman CSB

How much does God love you? As long as you're alive, you'll never be able to figure it out because God's love is just too big to comprehend. But this much we know: God loves you so much that He sent His Son Jesus to come to this earth and to die for you! And, when you accepted Jesus into your heart, God gave you a gift that is more precious than gold: the gift of eternal life.

Yes, God's love is bigger and more powerful than anybody can imagine, but His love is very real. So do yourself a favor right now: accept God's love with open arms and welcome His Son Jesus into your heart. When you do, your life will be changed today, tomorrow, and forever.

A bird does not know it can fly before it uses its wings. We learn God's love in our hearts as soon as we act upon it.

Corrie ten Boom

In Search of Answers

You will seek Me and find Me when you search for Me with all your heart.

—Jeremiah 29:13 Holman CSB

You've got questions? God's got answers. And if you'd like to hear from Him, here's precisely what you must do: petition Him with a sincere heart; be still; be patient; and listen. Then, in His own time and in His own fashion, God will answer your questions and give you guidance for the journey ahead.

Today, turn over everything to your Creator. Pray constantly about matters great and small. Seek God's instruction and His direction. And remember: God hears your prayers and answers them. But He won't answer the prayers that you don't get around to praying. So pray early and often. And then wait patiently for answers that are sure to come.

A prayerful heart and an obedient heart will learn, very slowly and not without sorrow, to stake everything on God Himself.

Elisabeth Elliot

What's Really Important

A pretentious, showy life is an empty life; a plain and simple life is a full life.

—Proverbs 13:7 MSG

Here's something to remember about stuff: It's not that important!

Lots of people are in love with money and the things that money can buy. God is not. God cares about people, not possessions, and so must you.

You should not be too concerned about the clothes you wear, or the things you own. And above all, don't ever let your self-esteem depend upon the things that you (or your parents) own.

The stuff that you own isn't nearly as important as the love that you feel in your heart—love for your family, love for your friends, and love for your Father in heaven.

What we possess often possesses us—we are possessed by possessions.

Oswald Chambers

I've learned to hold everything loosely because it hurts when God pries my fingers from it.

Corrie ten Boom

Your Good Deeds

Therefore by their fruits you will know them.

—Matthew 7:20 NKJV

English clergyman Thomas Fuller observed, "He does not believe who does not live according to his beliefs." These words are most certainly true. We may proclaim our beliefs to our hearts' content, but our proclamations will mean nothing—to others or to ourselves—unless we accompany our words with deeds that match. The sermons that we live are far more compelling than the ones we preach.

Like it or not, your life is an accurate reflection of your creed. If this fact gives you some cause for concern, don't bother talking about the changes that you intend to make—make them. And then, when your good deeds speak for themselves—as they most certainly will—don't interrupt.

Do nothing that you would not like to be doing when Jesus comes. Go no place where you would not like to be found when He returns.

Corrie ten Boom

Look to the Future, Not the Past

To You, O my Strength, I will sing praises; for God is my defense, my God of mercy.

—Psalm 59:17 NKJV

The old saying is familiar: "Forgive and forget." But when we have been hurt badly, forgiveness is often difficult and forgetting is downright impossible. Since we can't forget yesterday's troubles, we should learn from them. Yesterday has much to teach us about tomorrow. We may learn from the past, but we should never live in the past. God has given each of us a glorious day: this one. And it's up to each of us to use this day as faithful stewards.

So if you're trying to forget the past, don't waste your time. Instead, try a different approach: learn to accept the past and live in the present. Then, you can focus your thoughts and your energies, not on the troubles of yesterday, but instead on the profound opportunities that God has placed before you today.

Acceptance says: True, this is my situation at the moment. I'll look unblinkingly at the reality of it. But, I'll also open my hands to accept willingly whatever a loving Father sends me.

Catherine Marshall

Studying God's Word

As newborn babies want milk, you should want the pure and simple teaching. By it you can grow up and be saved.

—1 Peter 2:2 NCV

When it comes to your faith, God doesn't intend for you to stand still. He wants you to keep moving and growing. In fact, God's plan for you includes a lifetime of prayer, praise, and spiritual growth.

As a Christian, you should continue to grow in the love and the knowledge of your Savior as long as you live. How? By studying God's Word every day, by obeying His commandments, and by allowing His Son to reign over your heart, that's how.

Are you continually seeking to become a more mature believer? Hopefully so, because that's exactly what you owe to yourself and to God.

There is no way to draw closer to God unless you are in the Word of God every day. It's your compass. Your guide. You can't get where you need to go without it.

Stormie Omartian

When God Speaks Quietly

Speak, Lord. I am your servant and I am listening.

—1 Samuel 3:10 NCV

Sometimes God speaks loudly and clearly. More often, He speaks in a quiet voice—and if you are wise, you will be listening carefully when He does. To do so, you must carve out quiet moments each day to study His Word and sense His direction.

Can you quiet yourself long enough to listen to your conscience? And are you willing to pray sincerely and then to wait quietly for God's response. Hopefully so. Usually God refrains from sending His messages on stone tablets or city billboards. More often, He communicates in quieter ways. If you really desire to hear His voice, you must listen carefully, and you must do so in the silent corners of your quiet, willing heart.

Growth takes place in quietness, in hidden ways, in silence and solitude. The process is not accessible to observation.

Eugene Peterson

The world is full of noise. Might we not set ourselves to learn silence, stillness, solitude?

Elisabeth Elliot

Trust God and Think Positively

I am able to do all things through Him who strengthens me.
—Philippians 4:13 Holman CSB

Have you formed the habit of thinking positive thoughts? Hopefully so, because it's a wonderful habit to acquire. Once you learn to think positively about your world and yourself, you then put the self-fulfilling prophecy to work for you. Because you expect the best, you are much more likely to achieve the best.

You can control, to a surprising extent, the quality, the tone, and the direction of your thoughts. You can learn to prune out the negative ones and let the positive ones flourish. And that's precisely what you should learn to do.

So today, think optimistically about your life and your future. Trust your hopes, not your fears. Take time to celebrate God's glorious creation. And then, when you've filled your heart with hope and gladness, share your optimism with your friends. They'll be better for it, and so will you. But not necessarily in that order.

The Christian lifestyle is not one of legalistic do's and don'ts, but one that is positive, attractive, and joyful.

Vonette Bright

Walking with the Wise

Whoever walks with the wise will become wise; whoever walks with fools will suffer harm.

—Proverbs 13:20 NLT

Would you like to become very wise girl? Then you must walk with people who, by their words and their presence, make you wiser. And, you must try to avoid people who encourage you to think foolish thoughts or do foolish things.

Today, as a gift to yourself, select, from your friends and family members, a mentor whose judgment you trust. Then listen carefully to your mentor's advice and be willing to accept that advice, even if accepting it requires effort, or pain, or both. Consider your mentor to be God's gift to you. Thank God for that gift, and use it.

The effective mentor strives to help a man or woman discover what they can be in Christ and then holds them accountable to become that person.

Howard Hendricks

It takes a wise person to give good advice, but an even wiser person to take it.

Marie T. Freeman

Daily Distractions

If you decide for God, living a life of God-worship, it follows that you don't fuss about what's on the table at mealtimes or whether the clothes in your closet are in fashion. There is far more to your life than the food you put in your stomach, more to your outer appearance than the clothes you hang on your body.

—Matthew 6:25 MSG

This world is a complicated place, a place where things can get messed up in a hurry. So all of us must live through those days when the traffic jams, the computer crashes, and the dog makes a main course out of our homework. But, when we find ourselves distracted by the minor frustrations of life, we must catch ourselves, take a deep breath, and lift our thoughts upward.

Although we may, at times, struggle mightily to rise above the distractions of the everyday living, we need never struggle alone. God is here—eternal and faithful, with infinite patience and love—and, if we reach out to Him, He will restore our sense of perspective and give peace to our souls.

There is an enormous power in little things to distract our attention from God.

Oswald Chambers

A Future So Bright . . .

Wisdom is pleasing to you. If you find it, you have hope for the future.

—Proverbs 24:14 NCV

Let's talk for a minute about the future . . . your future. How bright do you believe your future to be? Well, if you're a faithful believer, God has plans for you that are so bright that you'd better pack several pairs of sunglasses and a lifetime supply of sun block!

The way that you think about your future will play a powerful role in determining how things turn out (it's called the "self-fulfilling prophecy," and it applies to everybody, including you). So here's another question: Are you expecting a terrific tomorrow, or are you dreading a terrible one? The answer to that question will have a powerful impact on the way tomorrow unfolds.

Today, as you live in the present and look to the future, remember that God has an amazing plan for you. Act—and believe—accordingly. And one more thing: don't forget the sun block.

You can look forward with hope, because one day there will be no more separation, no more scars, and no more suffering in My Father's House. It's the home of your dreams!

Anne Graham Lotz

God's Love

For the LORD your God has arrived to live among you. He is a mighty Savior. He will rejoice over you with great gladness. With his love, he will calm all your fears. He will exult over you by singing a happy song.

—Zephaniah 3:17 NLT

St. Augustine observed, "God loves each of us as if there were only one of us." Do you believe those words? Do you seek to have a real, one-on-one relationship with your Heavenly Father, or are you satisfied to keep Him at a "safe" distance?

Sometimes, in the crush of everyday life, God may seem far away, but He is not. God is everywhere we have ever been and everywhere we will ever go. He is with us night and day; He knows our thoughts and our prayers. And, when we earnestly seek Him, we will find Him because He is here, waiting patiently for us to reach out to Him.

Reach out to Him today, and accept His love.

Being loved by Him whose opinion matters most gives us the security to risk loving, too—even loving ourselves.

Gloria Gaither

Think Before You Speak

To everything there is a season…a time to keep silence, and a time to speak.

—Ecclesiastes 3:1, 7 KJV

Sometimes, it's easier to say the wrong thing than it is to say the right thing—especially if we're in a hurry to blurt out the first words that come into our heads. But, if we are patient and if we choose our words carefully, we can help other people feel better, and that's exactly what God wants us to do.

The Book of Proverbs tells us that the right words, spoken at the right time, can be wonderful gifts to our families and to our friends. That's why we should think about the things that we say before we say them, not after. When we do, our words make the world a better place, and that's exactly what God wants!

When you talk, choose the very same words that you would use if Jesus were looking over your shoulder. Because He is.

Marie T. Freeman

A little kindly advice is better than a great deal of scolding.

Fanny Crosby

Hope Now!

When dreams come true, there is life and joy.

—Proverbs 13:12 NLT

The hope that the world offers is fleeting and imperfect. The hope that God offers is unchanging, unshakable, and unending.

Where will you place your hopes today? Will you entrust your future to man or to God? Will you seek solace exclusively from fallible human beings, or will you place your hopes, first and foremost, in the trusting hands of your Creator? The decision is yours, and you must live with the results of the choice you make.

For thoughtful believers, hope begins with God. Period. So today, as you embark upon the next stage of your life's journey, consider the words of the Psalmist: "You are my hope; O Lord GOD, You are my confidence" (71:5 NASB). Then, place your trust in the One who cannot be shaken.

No other religion, no other philosophy promises new bodies, hearts, and minds. Only in the Gospel of Christ do hurting people find such incredible hope.

Joni Eareckson Tada

He's Number One

*Let us fix our eyes on Jesus, the author and perfecter of our faith,
who for the joy set before him endured the cross, scorning its
shame, and sat down at the right hand of the throne of God.*

—Hebrews 12:2 NIV

Okay, who is in charge of your heart? Is it God, or is
it something else? Have you given Christ your heart, your
soul, your talents, your time, and your testimony? Or are
you giving Him little more than a few hours each Sunday
morning?

In the book of Exodus, God warns that we should place
no gods before Him. Yet all too often, we place our Lord in
second, third, or fourth place as we worship other things.
When we unwittingly place possessions or relationships
above our love for the Creator, we create big problems for
ourselves.

Does God rule your heart? Make certain that the honest
answer to this question is a resounding yes. In the life of
every radical believer, God comes first. And that's precisely
the place that He deserves in your heart.

Make God's will the focus of your life day by day. If you seek
to please Him and Him alone, you'll find yourself satisfied
with life.

Kay Arthur

Growing with and Beyond Our Troubles

We also have joy with our troubles, because we know that these troubles produce patience. And patience produces character, and character produces hope.

—Romans 5:3-4 NCV

The next time Old Man Trouble knocks on your door, remember that he has lessons to teach. So turn away Mr. Trouble as quickly as you can, but as you're doing so, don't forget to learn his lessons. And remember: the trouble with trouble isn't just the trouble it causes; it's also the trouble we cause ourselves if we ignore the things that trouble has to teach. Got that? Then please don't forget it!

After all, a crisis doesn't make a person; it reveals what a person is made of.

Warren Wiersbe

If all struggles and sufferings were eliminated, the spirit would no more reach maturity than would the child.

Elisabeth Elliot

The Futility of Foolish Arguments

But stay away from those who have foolish arguments and talk about useless family histories and argue and quarrel about the law. Those things are worth nothing and will not help anyone.

—Titus 3:9 NCV

Arguments are seldom won but often lost. When we engage in petty squabbles, our losses usually outpace our gains. When we acquire the unfortunate habit of habitual bickering, we do harm to our friends, to our families, and to ourselves.

Time and again, God's Word warns us that most arguments are a monumental waste of time, of energy, of life. In Titus, we are warned to refrain from "foolish arguments," and with good reason. Such arguments usually do more for the devil than they do for God.

So the next time you're tempted to engage in a silly squabble, whether inside the church or outside it, refrain. When you do, you'll put a smile on God's face, and you'll send the devil packing.

When you "win" an argument, what have you really won? Not much!

Criswell Freeman

When You Do the Right Thing

His master replied, "Well done, good and faithful servant! You have been faithful with a few things; I will put you in charge of many things. Come and share your master's happiness!"

—Matthew 25:21 NIV

God has promised us this: when we do our duties in small matters, He will give us additional responsibilities. When we do our work dutifully, and when we behave responsibly, God rewards us—in a time and in a manner of His choosing, not our own.

Sometimes, God rewards us by giving us additional burdens to bear, or by changing the course of our lives so that we may better serve Him. Sometimes, our rewards come in the form of temporary setbacks that lead, in turn, to greater victories. Sometimes, God rewards us by answering "no" to our prayers so that He can say "yes" to a far grander request that we, with our limited understanding, would never have thought to ask for.

If you seek to be God's servant in great matters, be faithful, be patient, and be dutiful in smaller matters. Then step back and watch as God surprises you with the spectacular creativity of His infinite wisdom and His perfect plan.

God's Golden Rule

Just as you want others to do for you, do the same for them.
—Luke 6:31 Holman CSB

How should you treat other people? Jesus has the answer to that question. Jesus wants you to treat other people exactly like you want to be treated: with kindness, respect, and courtesy. When you do, you'll make your family and friends happy . . . and that's what God wants.

So if you're wondering how to treat someone else, follow the Golden Rule: treat the other people like you want them to treat you. When you do, you'll be obeying your Father in heaven and you'll be making other folks happy at the same time.

When we do little acts of kindness that make life more bearable for someone else, we are walking in love as the Bible commands us.

Barbara Johnson

Kindness in this world will do much to help others, not only to come into the light, but also to grow in grace day by day.

Fanny Crosby

Trust Your Heavenly Father

If God is for us, who is against us?

—Romans 8:31 Holman CSB

What do you expect from the day ahead? Are you expecting God to do wonderful things, or are you living beneath a cloud of fear and doubt? The familiar words of Psalm 118:24 remind us of a profound yet simple truth: "This is the day which the LORD hath made; we will rejoice and be glad in it" (KJV).

For thoughtful Christian girls (like you), every day begins and ends with God's Son and God's promises. When we accept Christ into our hearts, God promises us the opportunity for earthly peace and spiritual abundance. But more importantly, God promises us the priceless gift of eternal life.

As we face the inevitable challenges of life-here-on-earth, we must arm ourselves with the promises of God's Holy Word. When we do, we can expect the best, not only for the day ahead, but also for all eternity.

How changed our lives would be if we could only fly through the days on wings of surrender and trust!

Hannah Whitall Smith

Respect for Others

Being respected is more important than having great riches.

—Proverbs 22:1 ICB

Do you try to have a respectful attitude towards everybody? Hopefully so!

Should you be respectful of adults? Of course. Teachers? Certainly. Family members? Yes. Friends? Yep, but it doesn't stop there. The Bible teaches us to treat all people with respect.

Respect for others is habit-forming: the more you do it, the easier it becomes. So start practicing right now. Say lots of kind words and do lots of kind things, because when it comes to kindness and respect, practice makes perfect.

If you are willing to honor a person out of respect for God, you can be assured that God will honor you.

Beth Moore

It is the duty of every Christian to be Christ to his neighbor.

Martin Luther

Patience and Trust

Trust in him at all times, O people; pour out your hearts to him, for God is our refuge.

—Psalm 62:8 NIV

As individuals, as families, and as a nation, we are impatient for the changes that we so earnestly desire. We want solutions to our problems, and we want them right now! But sometimes, life's greatest challenges defy easy solutions, so we must be patient.

Psalm 37:7 commands us to "Rest in the Lord, and wait patiently for Him" (NKJV). But for most of us, waiting quietly for God is difficult. Why? Because we are imperfect beings who seek solutions to our problems today, if not sooner. We seek to manage our lives according to our own timetables, not God's. To do so is a mistake. Instead of impatiently tapping our fingers, we should fold our fingers and pray. When we do, our Heavenly Father will reward us in His own miraculous way and in His own perfect time.

Patience means waiting for God faithfully, hopefully, and prayerfully. But patience also means being willing to accept God's timetable, not our own.

Marie T. Freeman

His Promises Never Fail

Patient endurance is what you need now, so you will continue to do God's will. Then you will receive all that he has promised.

—Hebrews 10:36 NLT

God has made plenty of few promises to you, and He will most certainly keep them all. You can find these promises in the book God wrote. It's called the Bible, and you probably already own at least one or two copies.

The Bible is your guide for life here on earth and for life eternal—as a believer, you are called upon to trust its promises, to follow its commandments, and to share its Good News—beginning now and ending never.

There are four words I wish we would never forget, and they are, "God keeps his word."

Charles Swindoll

Fear and doubt are conquered by a faith that rejoices. And faith can rejoice because the promises of God are as certain as God Himself.

Kay Arthur

The Joy of Serving God

Enjoy serving the Lord, and he will give you what you want.
—Psalm 37:4 NCV

Are you a girl who is excited about serving God? You should be. As a believer living in today's challenging world, you have countless opportunities to honor your Father in Heaven by serving Him.

Far too many Christians seem bored with their faith and stressed by their service. Don't allow your self to become one of them! Serve God with thanksgiving in your heart and praise on your lips. Make your service to Him a time of celebration and thanksgiving. Worship your Creator by working for Him, joyfully, faithfully, and often.

God wants us to serve Him with a willing spirit, one that would choose no other way.

Beth Moore

If the attitude of servanthood is learned, by attending to God as Lord. Then, serving others will develop as a very natural way of life.

Eugene Peterson

Living in the Spirit of Truth

But when the Spirit of truth comes, he will lead you into all truth.

—John 16:13 NCV

God is vitally concerned with truth. His Word teaches the truth; His Spirit reveals the truth; His Son leads us to the truth. When we open our hearts to God, and when we allow His Son to rule over our thoughts and our lives, God reveals Himself, and we come to understand the truth about ourselves and the Truth about God's gift of grace.

The familiar words of John 8:32 remind us that "you shall know the truth, and the truth shall make you free" (NKJV). May we, as believers, seek God's truth and live by it, this day and forever.

Those who walk in truth walk in liberty.

Beth Moore

Truth will triumph. The Father of truth will win, and the followers of truth will be saved.

Max Lucado

Unreliable Thinking

Do not worry about anything, but pray and ask God for everything you need, always giving thanks.

—Philippians 4:6 NCV

Charles Swindoll advises, "When you're on the verge of throwing a pity party thanks to your despairing thoughts, go back to the Word of God." How true. Self-pity is not only an unproductive way to think, it is also an affront to your Father in Heaven.

God's Word promises that His children can receive abundance, peace, love, and eternal life. These gifts are not earned; they are an outpouring from God, a manifestation of His grace. With these rich blessings, how can we, as believers, feel sorry for ourselves? Self-pity and peace cannot coexist in the same mind. Bitterness and joy cannot coexist in the same heart. Thanksgiving and despair are mutually exclusive.

So, if your unreliable thoughts are allowing pain and worry to dominate your life, you must train yourself to think less about your troubles and more about God's blessings. When you stop to think about it, hasn't He given you enough blessings to occupy your thoughts all day, every day, from now on? Of course He has! So focus your mind on Him, and let your worries fend for themselves.

Words Speak Louder

In every way be an example of doing good deeds. When you teach, do it with honesty and seriousness.

—Titus 2:7 NCV

Our words speak, but our actions speak much more loudly. And whether we like it or not, all of us are role models. Our friends and family members observe our actions; as followers of Christ, we are obliged to act accordingly.

Corrie ten Boom advised, "Don't worry about what you do not understand. Worry about what you do understand in the Bible but do not live by." And that's sound advice because our families and friends are always watching . . . and so, for that matter, is God.

One of the best ways to witness to family, friends, and neighbors is to let them see the difference Jesus has made in your life.

Anne Graham Lotz

Among the most joyful people I have known have been some who seem to have had no human reason for joy. The sweet fragrance of Christ has shown through their lives.

Elisabeth Elliot

Practicing Forgiveness

Smart people know how to hold their tongue; their grandeur is to forgive and forget.

—Proverbs 19:11 MSG

If forgiveness were easy, everybody would be doing it. But forgiveness is hard, and it takes practice. Usually lots of practice. So when it comes to forgiveness, here's something you should remember: if at first you don't succeed, don't give up.

Are you having trouble forgiving someone (or, for that matter, forgiving yourself for a mistake that you've made)? If so, remember that, while forgiveness isn't easy, it isn't impossible, either. So keep trying until you get it right . . . and if you keep trying, you can be sure that sooner or later, you will find a way to forgive . . . and when you do, you'll be able to get on with your life.

Forgiveness is a stunning principle, your ticket out of hate and fear and chaos.

Barbara Johnson

If you're going to forgive somebody eventually, why wait?

Marie T. Freeman

The Joyful Life

Rejoice in the Lord always. I will say it again: Rejoice!
— Philippians 4:4 Holman CSB

C. S. Lewis once said, "Joy is the serious business of heaven." And he was right! God seriously wants you to be a seriously joyful person.

One way that you can have a more joyful life is by learning how to become a more obedient person. When you do, you'll stay out of trouble, and you'll have lots more time for fun.

So here's a way to be a more joyful, happy person: do the right thing! It's the best way to live.

Joy comes not from what we have but from what we are.

C. H. Spurgeon

Where the soul is full of peace and joy, outward surroundings and circumstances are of comparatively little account.

Hannah Whitall Smiith

Blessed Generosity

The one who blesses others is abundantly blessed; those who help others are helped.

—Proverbs 11:25 MSG

Jesus said, "It is more blessed to give than to receive." That means that we should be generous with other people—but sometimes we don't feel much like sharing. Instead of sharing the things that we have, we want to keep them all to ourselves. That's when we must remember that God doesn't want selfishness to rule our hearts; He wants us to be generous.

Are you blessed with enough stuff to share? If so, God's instructions are clear: you must share your blessings with others. And that's exactly the way it should be.

If you want to be truly happy, you won't find it on an endless quest for more stuff. You'll find it in receiving God's generosity and then passing that generosity along.

Bill Hybels

The measure of a life, after all, is not its duration but its donation.

Corrie ten Boom

Planning and Diligence

The plans of hard-working people earn a profit, but those who act too quickly become poor.

—Proverbs 21:5 NCV

Are you willing to plan for the future—and are you willing to work hard to accomplish the plans that you've made? The Book of Proverbs teaches that the plans of hardworking people (like you) are rewarded.

If you desire to reap a bountiful harvest from life, you must plan for the future while entrusting the final outcome to God. Then, you must do your part to make the future better (by working dutifully), while acknowledging the sovereignty of God's hands over all affairs, including your own.

Are you in a hurry for success to arrive at your doorstep? Don't be. Instead, work carefully, plan thoughtfully, and wait patiently. Remember that you're not the only one working on your behalf: God, too, is at work. And with Him as your partner, your ultimate success is guaranteed.

We can be victorious, but only if we walk with God.

Beth Moore

God Knows Best

However, each one must live his life in the situation the Lord assigned when God called him.

—1 Corinthians 7:17 Holman CSB

Here are three things to think about: 1. God loves you. 2. God wants what's best for you. 3. God has a plan for you.

God's plan may not always happen exactly like you want, but remember: God always knows best. Sometimes, even though you may want something very badly, you must still be patient and wait for the right time to get it, And the right time, of course, is determined by God.

Even if you don't get exactly what you want today, you can be sure that God wants what's best for you . . . today, tomorrow, and forever.

God isn't a talent scout looking for someone who is "good enough" or "strong enough." He is looking for someone with a heart set on Him, and He will do the rest.

Vance Havner

It's incredible to realize that what we do each day has meaning in the big picture of God's plan.

Bill Hybels

Shining Like Stars

The wise people will shine like the brightness of the sky. Those who teach others to live right will shine like stars forever and ever.

—Daniel 12:3 NCV

Our world needs Christian leaders who "will shine like stars forever and ever." Our world needs leaders who willingly honor God with their words and their deeds—with the emphasis on deeds.

If you seek to be a godly leader, then you must begin by being a worthy example to your family, to your friends, to your church, and to your community. After all, your words of instruction will never ring true unless you yourself are willing to follow them.

Are you the kind of leader whom you would want to follow? If so, congratulations. But if the answer to that question is no, then it's time to improve your leadership skills, beginning with the words that you speak and the example that you set. And the greatest of these, not surprisingly, is example.

People who inspire others are those who see invisible bridges at the end of dead-end streets.

Charles Swindoll

Sharing the Good News

Christ did not send me to baptize people but to preach the Good News. And he sent me to preach the Good News without using words of human wisdom so that the cross of Christ would not lose its power.

—1 Corinthians 1:17 NCV

A good way to build your faith is by talking about it—and that's precisely what God wants you to do. He wants you to share your faith.

In his second letter to Timothy, Paul shares a message to believers of every generation when he writes, "God has not given us a spirit of timidity" (1:7). Paul's meaning is clear: When sharing your testimony, you must be courageous and unashamed.

Let's face facts: You live in a world that desperately needs the healing message of Jesus Christ. Every believer, including you, bears responsibility for sharing the Good News. And it is important to remember that you give your testimony through your words and your actions. And, as the old saying goes, actions speak louder than words.

Choose Jesus Christ! Deny yourself, take up the Cross, and follow Him—for the world must be shown. The world must see, in us, a discernible, visible, startling difference.

Elisabeth Elliot

Concerning Stuff

Prosperity is as short-lived as a wildflower, so don't ever count on it.

—James 1:10 MSG

Are you a girl who's overly concerned with the stuff that money can buy? Hopefully not. On the grand stage of a well-lived life, material possessions should play a rather small role. Of course, we all need the basic necessities of life, but once we meet those needs for ourselves and for our families, the piling up of possessions creates more problems than it solves. Our real riches, of course, are not of this world. We are never really rich until we are rich in spirit.

Our society is in love with money and the things that money can buy. God is not. God cares about people, not possessions, and so must we. We must, to the best of our abilities, love our neighbors as ourselves, and we must, to the best of our abilities, resist the mighty temptation to place possessions ahead of people.

Money, in and of itself, is not evil; worshipping money is. So today, as you prioritize matters of importance in your life, remember that God is almighty, but the dollar is not.

Working with Heart and Soul

He was diligent in every deed that he began in the service of God's temple, in the law and in the commandment, in order to seek his God, and he prospered.

—2 Chronicles 31:21 Holman CSB

How does God intend for us to work? Does He intend for us to work diligently or does He, instead, reward mediocrity? The answer is obvious. God has created a world in which hard work is rewarded and sloppy work is not. Yet sometimes, we may seek ease over excellence, or we may be tempted to take shortcuts when God intends that we walk the straight and narrow path.

Today, heed God's Word by doing good work. Wherever you find yourself, whatever your job description, do your work, and do it with all your heart. When you do, you will most certainly win the recognition of your peers. But more importantly, God will bless your efforts and use you in ways that only He can understand. So do your work with focus and dedication. And leave the rest up to God.

Success or failure can be pretty well predicted by the degree to which the heart is fully in it.

John Eldredge

The Power of Positive Friendships

Light shines on those who do right; joy belongs to those who are honest. Rejoice in the Lord, you who do right. Praise his holy name.

—Psalm 97:11-12 NCV

If you'd like to build a positive life, find positive friends. If you'd like to live a godly life, seek the fellowship of godly friends. If you'd like to live passionately, prayerfully, and purposefully, spend time with people who are already living passionate, prayerful, purposeful lives. Soon, you'll discover that you will inevitably become more and more like the people who surround you day in and day out.

In choosing your friends, you set your course for the future. So choose carefully . . . very carefully.

The glory of friendship is not the outstretched hand, or the kindly smile, or the joy of companionship. It is the spiritual inspiration that comes to one when he discovers that someone else believes in him and is willing to trust him with his friendship.

Corrie ten Boom

Who Rules?

Do not worship any other gods besides me.

—Exodus 20:3 NLT

Who rules your heart? Is it God, or is it something else?

In the book of Exodus, God warns that we should place no gods before Him. Yet all too often, we place our Lord in second, third, or fourth place as we worship the gods of pride, greed, power, or personal gratification. When we unwittingly place possessions or relationships above our love for the Creator, we must seek His forgiveness and change our ways.

Does God rule your heart? Make certain that the honest answer to this question is a resounding yes. In the life of every righteous believer, God comes first. And that's precisely the place that He deserves in your heart.

A sense of deity is inscribed on every heart.

John Calvin

One with God is a majority.

Billy Graham

Stopping to Think

Knowing God leads to self-control. Self-control leads to patient endurance, and patient endurance leads to godliness.

—2 Peter 1:6 NLT

Maybe you're one of those girls who try to do everything fast, faster, or fastest! If so, maybe you sometimes do things before you think about the consequences of your actions. If that's the case, it's probably a good idea to slow down a little bit so you can think before you act. When you do, you'll soon discover the value of thinking carefully about things before you get started. And while you're at it, it's probably a good idea to think before you speak, too. After all, you'll never have to apologize for something that you didn't say.

Patience is the companion of wisdom.

St. Augustine

God does not give His counsel to the curious or the careless; He reveals His will to the concerned and to the consecrated.

Warren Wiersbe

Thanking God for His Gifts

Thanks be to God for his indescribable gift!

—2 Corinthians 9:15 NIV

How do we thank God for the gifts He has given us? By using those gifts, that's how!

God has given you talents and opportunities that are uniquely yours. Are you willing to use your gifts in the way that God intends? And are you willing to summon the discipline that is required to develop your talents and to hone your skills? That's precisely what God wants you to do, and that's precisely what you should desire for yourself.

As you seek to expand your talents, you will undoubtedly encounter stumbling blocks along the way, such as the fear of rejection or the fear of failure. When you do, don't stumble! Just continue to refine your skills, and offer your services to God. And when the time is right, He will use you—but it's up to you to be thoroughly prepared when He does.

What we are is God's gift to us. What we become is our gift to God.

Anonymous

Jesus Can Take Care of Our Problems

Do not love the world or the things that belong to the world. If anyone loves the world, love for the Father is not in him.

—1 John 2:15 Holman CSB

An old hymn contains the words, "This world is not my home; I'm just passing through." Thank goodness! This crazy world can be a place of trouble and danger. Thankfully, your real home is heaven, a place where you can live forever with Jesus.

In John 16:33, Jesus tells us He has overcome the troubles of this world. We should trust Him, and we should plan our days and our lives accordingly. When we do, we are forever blessed by the Son of God and His Father in heaven.

There is no hell on earth like horizontal living without God.

Charles Swindoll

The Lord Jesus Christ is still praying for us. He wants us to be in the world but not of it.

Charles Stanley

Obedience and Service

When all has been heard, the conclusion of the matter is: fear God and keep His commands.

—Ecclesiastes 12:13 Holman CSB

As you seek to discover God's purpose for your life, you may rest assured that His plan for you is centered around service to your family, to your friends, to your church, to your community, and to the world. God intends that you work diligently on His behalf to serve His children and to share His Good News.

Whom will you choose to serve today? The needs are great and the workers are few. And God is doing His very best to enlist able-bodied believers—like you.

The ultimate response to Jesus' teaching is belief and obedience.

John MacArthur

You may not always see immediate results, but all God wants is your obedience and faithfulness.

Vonette Bright

God Can Handle It

Now the God of all grace, who called you to His eternal glory in Christ Jesus, will personally restore, establish, strengthen, and support you.

—1 Peter 5:10 Holman CSB

Sometimes the future seems bright, and sometimes it does not. Yet even when we cannot see the possibilities of tomorrow, God can. As believers, our challenge is to trust an uncertain future to an all-powerful God.

When we trust God, we should trust Him completely. Can you place your future into the hands of a loving and all-knowing God? Can you live amid the uncertainties of today, knowing that God has dominion over all your tomorrows? If you can, you are wise and you are blessed. When you trust God with everything you are and everything you have, He will bless you now and forever.

All the power of God—the same power that hung the stars in place and put the planets in their courses and transformed Earth—now resides in you to energize and strengthen you to become the person God created you to be.

Anne Graham Lotz

Practical Christianity

My counsel for you is simple and straightforward: Just go ahead with what you've been given. You received Christ Jesus, the Master; now live him. You're deeply rooted in him. You're well constructed upon him. You know your way around the faith. Now do what you've been taught. School's out; quit studying the subject and start living it! And let your living spill over into thanksgiving.

—Colossians 2:6-7 MSG

As Christians, we must do our best to ensure that our actions are accurate reflections of our beliefs. Our theology must be demonstrated, not only by our words but, more importantly, by our actions. In short, we should be practical believers, quick to act whenever we see an opportunity to serve God.

Are you the kind of practical Christian girl who is willing to dig in and do what needs to be done when it needs to be done? If so, congratulations: God acknowledges your service and blesses it. But if you find yourself more interested in the fine points of theology than in the needs of your neighbors, it's time to rearrange your priorities. God needs believers who are willing to roll up their sleeves and go to work for Him. Count yourself among that number. Theology is a good thing unless it interferes with God's work. And it's up to you to make certain that your theology doesn't.

Our Intentions Are Important to God

We justify our actions by appearances; God examines our motives.

—Proverbs 21:2 MSG

Other people see you from the outside, and sometimes they judge you by the way you look. God, on the other hand, sees you from the inside—God sees your heart.

Kindness comes from the heart. So does love, caring, sharing, and obedience. These things are all important to God, far more important, in fact, than the way you appear to your friends and neighbors. So don't worry about looking good to the world. Worry, instead about looking good to God. He knows your heart, and He's far more concerned about your intentions and your motivations than He is about your outward appearance.

The more wisdom enters our hearts, the more we will be able to trust our hearts in difficult situations.

John Eldredge

Courage for Today . . . and Forever

Don't be afraid, because I am your God. I will make you strong and will help you; I will support you with my right hand that saves you.

—Isaiah 41:10 NCV

Christians have every reason to live courageously. After all, the ultimate battle has already been won on the cross at Calvary. But even dedicated followers of Christ may find their courage tested by the inevitable disappointments and fears that visit the lives of believers and non-believers alike.

When you find yourself worried about the challenges of today or the uncertainties of tomorrow, you must ask yourself whether or not you are ready to place your concerns and your life in God's all-powerful, all-knowing, all-loving hands. If the answer to that question is yes—as it should be—then you can draw courage today from the source of strength that never fails. That strength, of course, comes from: your Heavenly Father.

If a person fears God, he or she has no reason to fear anything else. On the other hand, if a person does not fear God, then fear becomes a way of life.

Beth Moore

Time for God

Anyone who comes to him [God] must believe that he exists and that he rewards those who earnestly seek him.

—Hebrews 11:6 NIV

When it comes to spending time with God, are you a "squeezer" or a "pleaser"? Do you squeeze God into your schedule with a prayer before mealtime, or do you please God by talking to Him far more often than that? If you're wise, you'll form the habit of spending time with God every day.

Even if you're the busiest person on Planet Earth, you can still carve out a little time for God. And when you think about it, isn't that the very least you should do?

Get reacquainted with God every day.

Criswell Freeman

I don't see how any Christian can survive, let alone live life as more than a conqueror, apart from a quiet time alone with God.

Kay Arthur

We all need to make time for God.
Even Jesus made time
to be alone with the Father.

—

Kay Arthur

Expecting Great Things

When a believing person prays, great things happen.
—James 5:16 NCV

James 5:16 makes a promise that God intends to keep: when you pray earnestly, fervently, and often, great things will happen. Too many people, however, are too timid or too pessimistic to ask God to do big things. Don't count yourself among their number.

God can and will do great things through you if you have the courage to ask Him and the determination to keep asking Him. Honor God by making big requests. But don't expect Him to do all the work. When you do your part, He will do His part. And when He does, expect a miracle . . . a big miracle.

We honor God by asking for great things when they are a part of His promise. We dishonor Him and cheat ourselves when we ask for molehills where He has promised mountains.

Vance Havner

God says we don't need to be anxious about anything; we just need to pray about everything.

Stormie Omartian

Wasted Words

A useless person causes trouble, and a gossip ruins friendships.
—Proverbs 16:28 NCV

Face it: gossip is bad—and the Bible clearly tells us that gossip is wrong.

When we say things that we don't want other people to know we said, we're being somewhat dishonest, but if the things we say aren't true, we're being very dishonest. Either way, we have done something that we may regret later, especially when the other person finds out.

The cost of gossip always exceeds its worth. So do yourself a big favor: don't talk about other people. It's a waste of words, and it's the wrong thing to do. You'll feel better about yourself if you don't gossip (and others will feel better about you, too). So don't do it!

To belittle is to be little.

Anonymous

Learning How to Forgive

Above all, keep your love for one another at full strength, since love covers a multitude of sins.

—1 Peter 4:8 Holman CSB

If you want to be an obedient Christian, you must be willing to forgive people. And, if you wish to build lasting relationships, you must learn how to forgive. Why? Because our loved ones are imperfect (as are we).

How often must we forgive our family and friends? More times than we can count . . . and that's exactly what God wants us to do.

Perhaps granting forgiveness is hard for you. If so, you are not the only girl on your block who has that challenge. Lasting forgiveness is often difficult to achieve—difficult but not impossible. Thankfully, with God's help, all things are possible, and that includes forgiveness. But, even though God is willing to help, He expects you to do some of the work. And make no mistake: forgiveness is work, which is okay with God. He knows that the payoffs are worth the effort.

God calls upon the loved not just to love but to be loving. God calls upon the forgiven not just to forgive but to be forgiving.

Beth Moore

Room to Grow

So let us stop going over the basics of Christianity again and again. Let us go on instead and become mature in our understanding.

—Hebrews 6:1 NLT

Are you a fully-grown person? Physically: maybe you're getting close. But spiritually? No way! And thank goodness that you're not! Even if you're very mature for your age, you've still got lots of room to grow.

The 19th-century writer Hannah Whitall Smith observed, "The maturity of a Christian experience cannot be reached in a moment." No kidding. In truth, the search for spiritual growth lasts a lifetime.

When we cease to grow, either emotionally or spiritually, we do ourselves and our families a profound disservice. But, if we study God's Word, if we obey His commandments, and if we live in the center of His will, we will not be "stagnant" believers; we will, instead, be growing Christians . . . and that's exactly what God wants for our lives. Come to think of it, that's exactly what you should want, too.

Keep your face upturned to Christ as the flowers do to the sun. Look, and your soul shall live and grow.

Hannah Whitall Smith

The Cheerful Giver

God loves the person who gives cheerfully.

—2 Corinthians 9:7 NLT

Are you one of those girls who is really a cheerful giver? If you intend to obey God's commandments, you will become the kind of girl you need to be. When you give, God looks not only at the quality of your gift, but also at the condition of your heart. If you give generously, joyfully, and without complaint, you obey God's Word. But, if you make your gifts grudgingly, or if the motivation for your gift is selfish, you're disobeying your Creator, and that's a big problem.

Today, take God's commandments to heart and make this pledge: Be a cheerful, generous, courageous giver. The world needs your help, and you need the spiritual rewards that will be yours when you give faithfully, prayerfully, and cheerfully.

How generous you are does not depend on how much you give, but how much you have left.

Anonymous

Getting to Know God

Stay clear of silly stories that get dressed up as religion. Exercise daily in God—no spiritual flabbiness, please!

—1 Timothy 4:7 MSG

Want to know God better? Then schedule a meeting with Him every day.

Each day has 1,440 minutes—will you spend a few of those minutes with your Heavenly Father? He deserves that much of your time and more. God wants you to pay attention to Him. So, if you haven't already done so, form the habit of spending quality time with your Creator. He deserves it . . . and so, for that matter, do you.

What digestion is to the body, meditation is to the soul.

Warren Wiersbe

How motivating it has been for me to view my early morning devotions as time of retreat alone with Jesus, Who desires that I "come with Him by myself to a quiet place" in order to pray, read His Word, listen for His voice, and be renewed in my spirit.

Anne Graham Lotz

The Power of Patience

Patience is better than strength. Controlling your temper is better than capturing a city.

—Proverbs 16:32 NCV

Temper tantrums are usually unproductive, unattractive, unforgettable, and unnecessary. Perhaps that's why Proverbs 16:32 states that, "Controlling your temper is better than capturing a city."

If you've allowed anger to become a regular visitor at your house, today you must pray for wisdom, for patience, and for a heart that is so filled with love and forgiveness that it contains no room for bitterness. God will help you terminate your tantrums if you ask Him to. And God can help you perfect your ability to be patient if you ask Him to. So ask Him, and then wait patiently for the ever-more-patient you to arrive.

When I am dealing with an all-powerful, all-knowing God, I, as a mere mortal, must offer my petitions not only with persistence, but also with patience. Someday I'll know why.

Ruth Bell Graham

The Wisdom of Thanksgiving

Give thanks to the Lord, for He is good; His faithful love endures forever.

—Psalm 106:1 Holman CSB

God's Word makes it clear: a wise heart is a thankful heart. Period. We are to worship God, in part, by the genuine gratitude we feel in our hearts for the marvelous blessings that our Creator has bestowed upon us. Yet even the most saintly among us must endure periods of bitterness, fear, doubt, and regret. Why? Because we are imperfect human beings who are incapable of perfect gratitude. Still, even on life's darker days, we must seek to cleanse our hearts of negative emotions and fill them, instead, with praise, with love, with hope, and with thanksgiving. To do otherwise is to be unfair to ourselves, to our loved ones, and to our God.

Don't have anything to be thankful for? Check your pulse!

Anonymous

Learning Life's Lessons . . . the Easy Way

Whoever is stubborn after being corrected many times will suddenly be hurt beyond cure.

—Proverbs 29:1 NCV

When it comes to learning life's lessons, we can either do things the easy way or the hard way. The easy way can be summed up as follows: when God teaches us a lesson, we learn it . . . the first time! Unfortunately, too many of us learn much more slowly than that.

When we resist God's instruction, He continues to teach, whether we like it or not. Our challenge, then, is to discern God's lessons from the experiences of everyday life. Hopefully, we learn those lessons sooner rather than later because the sooner we do, the sooner He can move on to the next lesson and the next, and the next . . .

We need to stop focusing on our lacks and stop giving out excuses and start looking at and listening to Jesus.

Anne Graham Lotz

The Positive Path

But the path of the just is like the shining sun, that shines ever brighter unto the perfect day. The way of the wicked is like darkness; they do not know what makes them stumble.

—Proverbs 4:18-19 NKJV

When Jesus addressed His disciples, He warned that each one must, "take up his cross and follow Me." The disciples must have known exactly what the Master meant. In Jesus' day, prisoners were forced to carry their own crosses to the location where they would be put to death. Thus, Christ's message was clear: in order to follow Him, Christ's disciples must deny themselves and, instead, trust Him completely. Nothing has changed since then.

If we are to be faithful disciples of the One from Galilee, we must trust Him and we must follow Him. Jesus never comes "next." He is always first. He shows us the path of life.

Do you seek to be a worthy disciple of Jesus? Then pick up His cross today and follow in His footsteps. When you do, you can walk with confidence: He will never lead you astray.

As you walk by faith, you live a righteous life, for righteousness is always by faith.

Kay Arthur

Life Is Great!

Rejoice in the Lord, you righteous ones; praise from the upright is beautiful.

—Psalm 33:1 Holman CSB

Life should never be taken for granted. Each day is a priceless gift from God and should be treated as such.

Hannah Whitall Smith observed, "How changed our lives would be if we could only fly through the days on wings of surrender and trust!" These words remind us that this day is God's creation, a gift to be treasured and enjoyed . . . starting now.

So if you're waiting for happiness to arrive at your doorstep "some day," wait no more. The best day to rejoice is this one.

We will never be happy until we make God the source of our fulfillment and the answer to our longings.

Stormie Omartian

Submit each day to God, knowing that He is God over all your tomorrows.

Kay Arthur

God's Instruction Book

Therefore, since we have this ministry, as we have received mercy, we do not give up. Instead, we have renounced shameful secret things, not walking in deceit or distorting God's message, but in God's sight we commend ourselves to every person's conscience by an open display of the truth.

—2 Corinthians 4:1-2 Holman CSB

God has given us a guidebook for righteous living called the Holy Bible. It contains thorough instructions which, if followed, lead to fulfillment, righteousness, and eternal life. But, if we choose to ignore God's commandments, the results are as predictable as they are tragic.

A righteous life has many components: faith, honesty, generosity, love, kindness, humility, gratitude, and worship, to name but a few. If we seek to follow the steps of our Savior, Jesus Christ, we must seek to live according to His commandments. In short, we must, to the best of our abilities, live according to the principles contained in God's Holy Word.

So today and every day of your life, study God's Word and live by it. Make your life a shining example for those who have not yet found Christ. Embrace righteousness.

And for further instructions, read the manual.

Returning God's Love . . . By Sharing It

My dear, dear friends, if God loved us like this, we certainly ought to love each other.

—1 John 4:11 MSG

God loves you. How will you respond to His love? The Bible clearly defines what your response should be: "You shall love the Lord your God with all your heart, with all your soul, and with all your strength" (Deuteronomy 6:5 NKJV). But you must not stop there. You must also love your neighbor as yourself. Jesus teaches that "On these two commandments hang all the Law and the Prophets" (Matthew 22:40).

Today, as you meet the demands of everyday living, will you pause long enough to return God's love? And then will you share it? Prayerfully, you will. When you embrace God's love, you are forever changed. When you embrace God's love, you feel differently about yourself, your family, your friends, and your world. When you embrace God's love, you have enough love to keep and enough love to share: enough love for a day, enough love for a lifetime, and enough love for all eternity.

God Is Love

For God so loved the world that he gave his only Son, so that everyone who believes in him will not perish but have eternal life.

—John 3:16 NLT

The Bible makes this promise: God is love. It's a big promise, a very important description of what God is and how God works. God's love is perfect. When we open our hearts to His love, we are blessed and we are protected.

Today, offer sincere prayers of thanksgiving to your Heavenly Father. He loves you now and throughout all eternity. Open your heart to His presence and His love.

No part of our prayers creates a greater feeling of joy than when we praise God for who He is. He is our Master Creator, our Father, our source of all love.

Shirley Dobson

I am convinced our hearts are not healthy until they have been satisfied by the only completely healthy love that exists: the love of God Himself.

Beth Moore

A Perfect Timetable

He has made everything appropriate in its time. He has also put eternity in their hearts, but man cannot discover the work God has done from beginning to end.

—Ecclesiastes 3:11 Holman CSB

Of this you can be sure: God's sense of timing is without error. God's timing may not coincide with your preferred timing—which, by the way, is perfectly fine with God because He knows precisely what He's doing, even if you may not.

Perhaps you're impatient for God to reveal His plans for your life. If so, it is time to reread the third chapter of Ecclesiastes. Solomon's words will remind you that there is a time for every purpose under God's heaven—and that includes your purpose.

When we read of the great Biblical leaders, we see that it was not uncommon for God to ask them to wait, not just a day or two, but for years, until God was ready for them to act.

Gloria Gaither

Giving an Account of Ourselves

Yes, each of us will have to give a personal account to God.
—Romans 14:12 NLT

For most of us, it can be a scary thought: one day, we'll come face-to-face with our Heavenly Father, and we'll be called to account for our actions here on earth. Our personal histories will certainly not be surprising to God; He already knows everything about us. But the full scope of our activities may be surprising to us: some of us will be pleasantly surprised; others will not be.

Today and every day, be a wise girl—do whatever you can to ensure that your thoughts and your deeds are pleasing to your Creator. After all, at some point in the future, you will most certainly be called to account for your actions. And the future may be sooner than you think.

Don't worry about what you do not understand. Worry about what you do understand in the Bible but do not live by.

Corrie ten Boom

Patience with Others and One's Self

God has chosen you and made you his holy people. He loves you. So always do these things: Show mercy to others, be kind, humble, gentle, and patient.

—Colossians 3:12 NCV

The dictionary defines the word patience as "the ability to be calm, tolerant, and understanding." If that describes you, you can skip the rest of this page. But, if you're like most of us, you'd better keep reading.

For most of us, patience is a hard thing to master. Why? Because we have lots of things we want, and we want them NOW (if not sooner). But the Bible tells us that we must learn to wait patiently for the things that God has in store for us.

The next time you find your patience tested to the limit, remember that the world unfolds according to God's timetable, not yours. Sometimes, you must wait patiently, and that's as it should be. After all, think how patient God has been with you!

The times we find ourselves having to wait on others may be the perfect opportunities to train ourselves to wait on the Lord.

Joni Eareckson Tada

You're Unique

Blessed is the man who does not condemn himself.
—Romans 14:22 Holman CSB

When God made you, He made you in a very special way. In fact, you're a wonderful, one-of-a-kind creation, a special girl unlike any other.

Do you realize how special you are? Do you know that God loves you because of who you are (not because of the things you've done)? And do you know that God has important work for you to do? Well whether you realize it or not, all these things are all true.

So the next time you feel bad about something you've done, take a look in the mirror, and remember that you're looking at a wonderfully special person . . . you!

God loves you . . . and that's the way that you should feel about yourself, too.

If you can forgive the person you were, accept the person you are, and believe in the person you will become, you are headed for joy. So celebrate your life.

Barbara Johnson

His Plans . . . and Yours

There is no wisdom, understanding, or advice that can succeed against the Lord.

—Proverbs 21:30 NCV

Does God have a plan for your life? Of course He does! Every day of your life, He is trying to lead you along a path of His choosing . . . but He won't force you to follow. God has given you free will, the opportunity to make decisions for yourself. The choices are yours: either you will choose to obey His Word and seek His will, or you will choose to follow a different path.

God's plans for you may be far bigger than you imagine, but He may be waiting for you to make the next move—so today, make that move prayerfully, faithfully, and expectantly. And after you've made your move, trust God to make His.

Almost 2,000 years ago, Jesus Christ won the decisive battle against sin and Satan through His death and resurrection. Satan did his best to defeat God's plans, but he could not win against God's overwhelming power.

Billy Graham

God Has Plans for You

If we live by the Spirit, we must also follow the Spirit.
—Galatians 5:25 Holman CSB

God has plans for your life, wonderful, surprising plans . . . but He won't force those plans upon you. To the contrary, He has given you free will, the ability to make decisions on your own. Now, it's up to you to make those decisions wisely.

If you seek to live in accordance with God's plan for your life, you will study His Word, you will be attentive to His instructions, and you will be watchful for His signs. You will associate with fellow believers who, by their words and actions, will encourage your spiritual growth. You will assiduously avoid those two terrible temptations: the temptation to sin and the temptation to squander time. And finally, you will listen carefully, even reverently, to the conscience that God has placed in your heart.

God intends to use you in wonderful, unexpected ways if you let Him. Let Him. When you do, you'll be thoroughly surprised by the creativity and the beauty of His plans.

His life is our light—our purpose and meaning and reason for living.

Anne Graham Lotz

Godly Thoughts, Godly Actions

Commit your activities to the Lord and your plans will be achieved.

—Proverbs 16:3 Holman CSB

Our thoughts have the power to lift us up or drag us down; they have the power to energize us or deplete us, to inspire us to greater accomplishments, or to make those accomplishments impossible.

God intends that you experience joy and abundance, but He will not impose His joy upon you; you must accept it for yourself. It's up to you to celebrate the life that God has given you by focusing your mind upon "whatever is of good repute" (Philippians 4:8). So today, spend more time thinking about God's blessings, and less time fretting about the minor inconveniences of life. Then, take time to thank the Giver of all things good for gifts that are glorious, miraculous, and eternal.

People who do not develop and practice good thinking often find themselves at the mercy of their circumstances.

John Maxwell

The Power of Willing Hands

A lazy person will end up poor, but a hard worker will become rich.

—Proverbs 10:4 NCV

God's Word teaches us the value of hard work. In his second letter to the Thessalonians, Paul warns, "…if anyone will not work, neither shall he eat" (3:10 NKJV). And the Book of Proverbs proclaims, "A person who doesn't work hard is just like someone who destroys things" (18:9 NCV). In short, God has created a world in which diligence is rewarded but sloth is not. So, whatever it is that you choose to do, do it with enthusiasm and dedication.

Hard work is not simply a proven way to get ahead, it's also part of God's plan for you. God did not create you for a life of mediocrity; He created you for far greater things. Reaching for greater things usually requires work and lots of it, which is perfectly fine with God. After all, He knows that you're up to the task, and He has big plans for you if you possess a loving heart and willing hands.

You can't climb the ladder of life with your hands in your pockets.

Barbara Johnson

Faithfulness and Focus

But if from there you seek the LORD your God, you will find him if you look for him with all your heart and with all your soul.

—Deuteronomy 4:29 NIV

God deserves your best. Is He getting it? Do you make an appointment with your Heavenly Father each day? Do you carve out moments when He receives your undivided attention? Or is your devotion to Him fleeting, distracted, and sporadic?

When you acquire the habit of focusing your heart and mind squarely upon God's intentions for your life, He will guide your steps and bless your endeavors. But if you allow distractions to take priority over your relationship with God, they will—and you will pay a price for your mistaken priorities.

Today, focus upon God's Word and upon His will for your life. When you do, you'll be amazed at how quickly everything else comes into focus, too.

Success isn't the key. Faithfulness is.

Joni Eareckson Tada

Understanding Christ's Love

And I pray that you and all God's holy people will have the power to understand the greatness of Christ's love—how wide and how long and how high and how deep that love is. Christ's love is greater than anyone can ever know, but I pray that you will be able to know that love. Then you can be filled with the fullness of God.

—Ephesians 3:18–19 NCV

Christ's love for you is personal. He loves you so much that He gave His life in order that you might spend all eternity with Him. Christ loves you individually and intimately; His is a love unbounded by time or circumstance. Are you willing to experience an intimate relationship with Him? Your Savior is waiting patiently; don't make Him wait a single minute longer. Embrace His love today. Fill yourself with the fullness of God.

Christ is like a river that is continually flowing. There are always fresh supplies of water coming from the fountainhead, so that a man may live by it and be supplied with water all his life. They who live upon Christ may have fresh supplies from him for all eternity.

Jonathan Edwards

The Time Is Now

Hard work means prosperity; only fools idle away their time.
—Proverbs 12:11 NLT

Are you one of those girls who put things off until the last minute? Do you waste time doing things that don't matter very much while putting off the important things until it's too late to do the job right? If so, it's now time to start making better choices.

It may seem like you've got all the time in the world to do the things you need to do, but time is shorter than you think. Time here on earth is limited . . . use it or lose it!

Our time is short! The time we can invest for God, in creative things, in receiving our fellowmen for Christ, is short!

Billy Graham

Never fail to do something because you don't feel like it. Sometimes you just have to do it now, and you'll feel like it later.

Marie T. Freeman

Faith on Fire

I tell you the truth, whoever believes in me will do the same things that I do. Those who believe will do even greater things than these, because I am going to the Father.

—John 14:12 NCV

John Wesley advised, "Catch on fire with enthusiasm and people will come for miles to watch you burn." His words still ring true. When we fan the flames of enthusiasm for Christ, our faith serves as a beacon to others.

Our world desperately needs faithful believers who share the Good News of Jesus with joyful exuberance. Be such a believer. The world desperately needs your enthusiasm, and just as importantly, you need the experience of sharing it.

One of the great needs in the church today is for every Christian to become enthusiastic about his faith in Jesus Christ.

Billy Graham

Enthusiasm, like the flu, is contagious—we get it from one another.

Barbara Johnson

Beyond Blame

When they continued to ask Jesus their question, he raised up and said, "Anyone here who has never sinned can throw the first stone at her."

—John 8:7 NCV

To blame others for our own problems isn't smart. Yet blaming others is so easy to do and improving ourselves is so much harder. So instead of solving problems ourselves, we are tempted to do otherwise; we are tempted to fret over the perceived unfairness of life while doing precious little else.

Are you looking for an ironclad formula for problem-solving that will leave you happier, healthier, wealthier, and wiser? Here it is: don't play the blame game—because to play it is to lose it.

You'll never win the blame game, so why even bother to play?

Marie T. Freeman

The main thing is this:
we should never blame anyone or
anything for our defeats.
No matter how evil their intentions
may be, they are altogether unable
to harm us until we begin to blame
them and use them as excuses
for our own unbelief.

———

A. W. Tozer

Fairness and Honest Dealings

The Lord hates dishonest scales, but he is pleased with honest weights.

—Proverbs 11:1 NCV

It has been said on many occasions and in many ways that honesty is the best policy. For believers, it is far more important to note that honesty is God's policy. And if we are to be servants worthy of our Savior, Jesus Christ, we must be honest and forthright in our communications with others.

Sometimes, honesty is difficult; sometimes, honesty is painful; always, honesty is God's commandment. In the Book of Exodus, God did not command, "Thou shalt not bear false witness when it is convenient." And He didn't say, "Thou shalt not bear false witness most of the time." God said, "Thou shalt not bear false witness against thy neighbor." Period.

Sometime soon, perhaps even today, you will be tempted to bend the truth or perhaps even to break it. Resist that temptation. Truth is God's way...and it must also be yours. Period.

Got Questions?

An indecisive man is unstable in all his ways.

—James 1:8 Holman CSB

God doesn't explain Himself to us with the clarity that we humans would prefer (think about this: if God did explain Himself with perfect clarity, we wouldn't have enough brainpower to understand the explanation that He gave!).

When innocent people are hurt, we question God because we can't figure out exactly what He's doing, or why. Since we can't fully answer that question now, we must trust in God's love, God's wisdom, and God's plan.

And while we're waiting for that wonderful day when all our questions will be answered (in heaven), we should use the time that we have here on earth to help the people who need it most.

Be to the world a sign that while we as Christians do not have all the answers, we do know and care about the questions.

Billy Graham

Enough Is Enough

Let your character be free from the love of money, being content with what you have; for He Himself has said, "I will never desert you, nor will I ever forsake you."

—Hebrews 13:5 NASB

Ours is a world that glorifies material possessions. Christians, of course, should not. As believers who have been touched and transformed by the grace of a risen Savior, we must never allow the things of this earth to distance us from our sense of God's presence and the direction of God's hand. If we are to enjoy the peace and abundance that God has promised us, we must reign in our desire for more and more; we must acknowledge that when it comes to earthly possessions, enough is always enough.

The key to contentment is to consider. Consider who you are and be satisfied with that. Consider what you have and be satisfied with that. Consider what God's doing and be satisfied with that.

Luci Swindoll

True contentment comes from godliness in the heart, not from wealth in the hand.

Warren Wiersbe

The Love of Money . . .

For the love of money is a root of all sorts of evil, and some by longing for it have wandered away from the faith and pierced themselves with many griefs. But flee from these things, you man of God, and pursue righteousness, godliness, faith, love, perseverance and gentleness.

—1 Timothy 6:11 NASB

Our society is in love with money and the things that money can buy. God is not. God cares about people, not possessions, and so must we. We must, to the best of our abilities, love our neighbors as ourselves, and we must, to the best of our abilities, resist the mighty temptation to place possessions ahead of people.

Money, in and of itself, is not evil; worshipping money is. So today, as you prioritize matters of importance for you and yours, remember that God is almighty, but the dollar is not. If we worship God, we are blessed. But if we worship "the almighty dollar," we are inevitably punished because of our misplaced priorities—and our punishment usually comes sooner rather than later.

Our ultimate aim in life is not to be healthy, wealthy, prosperous, or problem free. Our ultimate aim in life is to bring glory to God.

Anne Graham Lotz

Your Parents Can Help You Be Successful

Success, success to you, and success to those who help you, for your God will help you....

—1 Chronicles 12:18 NIV

God makes this promise: If you have faith in Him, you can do BIG things! So if you have something important to do, pray about it and ask God for help. When you ask God to help you, He will. And while you're at it, never be afraid to ask your parents for their help, too.

When you talk things over with your parents, you'll soon discover that they want you to do BIG things . . . and they can give you LOTS of help along the way.

Success and happiness are not destinations. They are exciting, never-ending journeys.

Zig Ziglar

Success or failure can be pretty well predicted by the degree to which the heart is fully in it.

John Eldredge

Worshipping Christ

He is not here, but He has been resurrected!

—Luke 24:6 Holman CSB

God has a wonderful plan for your life, and an important part of that plan includes worship. We should never deceive ourselves: every life is based upon some form of worship. The question is not whether we worship, but what we worship.

Some of us choose to worship God. The result is a plentiful harvest of joy, peace, and abundance. Others distance themselves from God by foolishly worshiping earthly possessions and personal gratification. To do so is a mistake of profound proportions.

Have you accepted the grace of God's only begotten Son? Then worship Him. Worship Him today and every day. Worship Him with sincerity and thanksgiving. Write His name on your heart and rest assured that He, too, has written your name on His.

When we are in a situation where Jesus is all we have, we soon discover he is all we really need.

Gigi Graham Tchividjian

Only One You

To acquire wisdom is to love oneself; people who cherish understanding will prosper.

—Proverbs 19:8 NLT

Do you really like the person you see when you look into the mirror? You should! After all, the person in the mirror is a very special person who is made—and loved—by God.

In fact, you are loved in many, many ways: God loves you, your parents love you, and your family loves you, for starters. So you should love yourself, too.

So here's something to think about: since God thinks you're special, and since so many people think you're special, isn't it about time for you to agree with them? Of course it is! It's time to say, "You're very wonderful and very special," to the person you see in the mirror.

Your self worth is more important than your net worth.

Anonymous

Beyond Anxiety

Anxiety in a man's heart weighs it down, but a good word cheers it up.

—Proverbs 12:25 Holman CSB

God calls us to live above and beyond our worries. God calls us to live by faith, not by fear. He instructs us to trust Him completely, this day and forever. But sometimes, trusting God is difficult, especially when we become caught up in the incessant demands of an anxious world.

When you feel anxious—and you will—return your thoughts to God's love. Then, take your concerns to Him in prayer, and to the best of your ability, leave them there. Whatever "it" is, God is big enough to handle it. Let Him. Now.

The thing that preserves a man from panic is his relationship to God.

Oswald Chambers

We must lay our questions, frustrations, anxieties, and impotence at the feet of God and wait for His answer. And then receiving it, we must live by faith.

Kay Arthur

Never Give Up

Even though good people may be bothered by trouble seven times, they are never defeated.

—Proverbs 24:16 NCV

Do you sincerely want to live a life that is pleasing to God? If so, you must remember that life is not a sprint, it's a marathon that calls for preparation, determination, and lots of perseverance.

Are you one of those people who doesn't give up easily, or are you quick to bail out when the going gets tough? If you've developed the unfortunate habit of giving up at the first sign of trouble, it's probably time for you to have a heart-to-heart talk with the girl you see every time you look in the mirror.

If you're facing a difficult situation, remember this: whatever your problem, God can handle it. Your job is to keep persevering until He does.

Determination and faithfulness are the nails used to build the house of God's dreams.

Barbara Johnson

Contentment Now

Your life should be free from the love of money. Be satisfied with what you have, for He Himself has said, I will never leave you or forsake you.

—Hebrews 13:5 Holman CSB

Where can we find contentment? Is it a result of being wealthy or famous? Nope. Genuine contentment is a gift from God to those who trust Him and follow His commandments.

If we don't find contentment in God, we will never find it anywhere else. But, if we seek Him and obey Him, we will be blessed with joyful, peaceful, meaningful lives. When God dwells at the center of our lives, peace and contentment will belong to us just as surely as we belong to God.

You've heard the saying, "Life is what you make it." That means we have a choice. We can choose to have a life full of frustration and fear, but we can just as easily choose one of joy and contentment.

Dennis Swanberg

Guarding Our Hearts and Minds

Summing it all up, friends, I'd say you'll do best by filling your minds and meditating on things true, noble, reputable, authentic, compelling, gracious, the best, not the worst; the beautiful, not the ugly; things to praise, not things to curse. Put into practice what you learned from me, what you heard and saw and realized. Do that, and God, who makes everything work together, will work you into his most excellent harmonies.

—Philippians 4:8-9 MSG

You are near and dear to God. He loves you more than you can imagine, and He wants the very best for you. And one more thing: God wants you to guard your heart.

Every day, you are faced with choices . . . lots of them. You can do the right thing, or not. You can tell the truth, or not. You can be kind, and generous, and obedient. Or not.

Your mind and your heart will usually tell you the right thing to do. And if you listen to your parents and grandparents, they will help you, too, by teaching you God's rules. Then, you will learn that doing the right thing is always better than doing the wrong thing. And, by obeying God's rules, you will guard your heart by giving it to His Son Jesus.

Look Before You Leap

An impulsive vow is a trap; later you'll wish you could get out of it.

—Proverbs 20:25 MSG

Are you, at times, just a little bit too impulsive for your own good? Do you sometimes fail to look before you leap? If so, God wants to have a little chat with you.

God's Word is clear: as believers, we are called to lead lives of discipline, diligence, moderation, and maturity. But the world often tempts us to behave otherwise. Everywhere we turn, or so it seems, we are faced with powerful temptations to behave in undisciplined, ungodly ways.

God's Word instructs us to be disciplined in our thoughts and our actions; God's Word warns us against the dangers of impulsive behavior. As believers in a just God, we should act and react accordingly.

In times of uncertainty, wait. Always, if you have any doubt, wait. Do not force yourself to any action. If you have a restraint in your spirit, wait until all is clear, and do not go against it.

Mrs. Charles E. Cowman

What God Requires

But he's already made it plain how to live, what to do, what God is looking for in men and women. It's quite simple: Do what is fair and just to your neighbor, be compassionate and loyal in your love, and don't take yourself too seriously—take God seriously.

—Micah 6:8 MSG

When Jesus was tempted by Satan, the Master's response was clear. Jesus chose to worship the Lord and serve Him only. We, as followers of Christ, must follow in His footsteps.

When we place God in a position of secondary importance, we do ourselves great harm and we put ourselves at great risk. But when we place God squarely in the center of our lives—when we walk humbly and obediently with Him—we are blessed and we are protected.

If you aren't serving, you're just existing, because life is meant for ministry.

Rick Warren

Through our service to others, God wants to influence our world for Him.

Vonette Bright

Wisdom Is as Wisdom Does

A foolish person enjoys doing wrong, but a person with understanding enjoys doing what is wise.

—Proverbs 10:23 NCV

Do you want to become a really wise girl? If so, you must behave wisely. Wisdom is as wisdom does.

High-sounding platitudes are as common as table salt. Aphorisms are everywhere. Parables proliferate. No matter. Wisdom is denominated not by words, but by deeds.

Do you wish to walk among the wise? If so, you must walk wisely. There is simply no other way.

The doorstep to the temple of wisdom is a knowledge of our own ignorance.

C. H. Spurgeon

If we neglect the Bible, we cannot expect to benefit from the wisdom and direction that result from knowing God's Word.

Vonette Bright

Be Thankful Now!

And whatever you do, in word or in deed, do everything in the name of the Lord Jesus, giving thanks to God the Father through Him.

—Colossians 3:17 Holman CSB

Do you have a thankful attitude? Hopefully so! After all, you've got plenty of things to be thankful for. Even during those times when you're angry or tired, you're a very lucky person.

Who has given you all the blessings you enjoy? Your parents are responsible, of course. But all of your blessings really start with God. That's why you should say "Thank You" to God many times each day. He's given you so much . . . so thank Him, starting now.

It is only with gratitude that life becomes rich.

Dietrich Bonhoeffer

God has promised that if we harvest well with the tools of thanksgiving, there will be seeds for planting in the spring.

Gloria Gaither

Living in an Anxious World

Don't fret or worry. Instead of worrying, pray. Let petitions and praises shape your worries into prayers, letting God know your concerns. Before you know it, a sense of God's wholeness, everything coming together for good, will come and settle you down. It's wonderful what happens when Christ displaces worry at the center of your life.

—Philippians 4:6-7 MSG

We live in a world that often breeds anxiety and fear. When we come face-to-face with tough times, we may fall prey to discouragement, doubt, or depression. But our Father in Heaven has other plans. God has promised that we may lead lives of abundance, not anxiety. In fact, His Word instructs us to "be anxious for nothing." But how can we put our fears to rest? By taking those fears to God and leaving them there.

As you face the challenges of everyday living, do you find yourself becoming anxious, troubled, discouraged, or fearful? If so, turn every one of your concerns over to your Heavenly Father. The same God who created the universe will comfort you if you ask Him…so ask Him and trust Him. And then watch in amazement as your anxieties melt into the warmth of His loving hands.

Loving God, Loving People

Jesus replied, "'Love the Lord your God with all your heart and with all your soul and with all your mind.' This is the first and greatest commandment. And the second is like it: 'Love your neighbor as yourself.' All the Law and the Prophets hang on these two commandments."

—Matthew 22:37-40 NIV

Christ's words are clear: He instructs us to love the Lord with all our hearts and to love our neighbors as we love ourselves. But sometimes, despite our best intentions, we fall short. When we become embittered with ourselves, with our neighbors, or most especially with God, we disobey the One who gave His life for us. And we bring inevitable, needless suffering into our lives.

In 1 Corinthians 13, we are told that love is the foundation upon which all our relationships are to be built—our relationships with others and our relationship with our Creator. May we fill our hearts with love; may we never yield to bitterness. And may we praise the Son of God who, in His infinite wisdom, made love His greatest commandment.

I love Him because He first loved me, and He still does love me, and He will love me forever and ever.

Bill Bright

Big Rewards When You Do the Right Thing

Do you want to be counted wise, to build a reputation for wisdom? Here's what you do: Live well, live wisely, live humbly. It's the way you live, not the way you talk, that counts.

—James 3:13 MSG

If you open up a dictionary, you'll see that the word "wisdom" means "using good judgment, and knowing what is true." But there's more to it than that. It's not enough to know what's right—if you want to be wise, you must also do what's right.

The Bible promises that when you do smart things, you'll earn big rewards (and it also promises, by the way, that if you do dumb things, you definitely won't get big rewards).

So slow down and think about things before you do them, not after. It's the smart way to live.

Let us not be content to wait and see what will happen, but give us the determination to make the right things happen.

Peter Marshall

That Little Voice

For God is pleased with you when, for the sake of your conscience, you patiently endure unfair treatment.

—1 Peter 2:19 NLT

When you know that you're doing what's right, you'll feel better about yourself. Why? Because you have a little voice in your head called your conscience. Your conscience is the feeling that tells you whether something is right or wrong—and it's a feeling that makes you feel better about yourself when you know you've done the right thing.

Your conscience is an important tool. Pay attention to it! The more you listen to your conscience, the easier it is to behave yourself.

So here's great advice: first, slow down long enough to figure out the right thing to do—and then do it! When you do, you'll be very glad you did.

One's conscience can only be satisfied when God is satisfied.

C. H. Spurgeon

Be Humble

We love because He first loved us.

—1 John 4:19 Holman CSB

As we consider Christ's sacrifice on the cross, we should be profoundly humbled. And today, as we come to Christ in prayer, we should do so in a spirit of humble devotion.

Jesus humbled Himself on a cross—for you. He shed His blood—for you. He has offered to walk with you through this life and throughout all eternity. As you approach Him today in prayer, think about His sacrifice and His grace. And be humble.

Do you wish to be great? Then begin by being humble. Do you desire to construct a vast and lofty fabric? Think first about the foundations of humility. The higher your structure is to be, the deeper must be its foundation.

St. Augustine

If you know who you are in Christ, your personal ego is not an issue.

Beth Moore

On Guard Against Evil

Your love must be real. Hate what is evil, and hold on to what is good.

—Romans 12:9 NCV

Face facts: this world is inhabited by quite a few people who are very determined to do evil things. The devil and his human helpers are working 24/7 to cause pain and heartbreak in every corner of the globe . . . including your corner. So you'd better beware.

Your job, if you choose to accept it, is to recognize evil and fight it. The moment that you decide to fight evil whenever you see it, you can no longer be a lukewarm, halfhearted Christian. And, when you are no longer a lukewarm Christian, God rejoices while the devil despairs.

When will you choose to get serious about fighting the evils of our world? Before you answer that question, consider this: in the battle of good versus evil, the devil never takes a day off . . . and neither should you.

Light is stronger than darkness—darkness cannot "comprehend" or "overcome" it.

Anne Graham Lotz

The Right Thing

For the Kingdom of God is not just fancy talk; it is living by God's power.

—1 Corinthians 4:20 NLT

Doing the right thing is not always easy, especially when we're tired or frustrated. But, doing the wrong thing almost always leads to trouble. And sometimes, it leads to BIG trouble.

When you do the right thing, you don't have to worry about what you did or what you said. But, if you are dishonest—or if you do something that you know is wrong—you'll be worried that someone will find out. So do the right thing; it may be harder in the beginning, but it's easier in the end.

Life is a series of choices between the bad, the good, and the best. Everything depends on how we choose.

Vance Havner

Our walk counts far more than our talk, always!

George Mueller

Wisdom from Above

The Lord says, "I will make you wise and show you where to go. I will guide you and watch over you."

—Psalm 32:8 NCV

Your head is undoubtedly filled with a growing collection of valuable information. But, there is much yet to learn. Wisdom is like a savings account: If you add to it consistently, then eventually you'll have a great sum. The secret to success is consistency.

Would you like to become a little wiser every day? Then keep learning. Seek wisdom now, and seek it in the right place. That place, of course, is, first and foremost, the Word of God. And remember this: it's not enough to simply read God's Word; you've also got to live by it. No exceptions!

If we neglect the Bible, we cannot expect to benefit from the wisdom and direction that result from knowing God's Word.

Vonette Bright

Contagious Christianity

All those who stand before others and say they believe in me, I will say before my Father in heaven that they belong to me.

—Matthew 10:32 NCV

Genuine, heartfelt Christianity is contagious. If you enjoy a life-altering relationship with God, that relationship will have an impact on others—perhaps a very big impact.

Are you genuinely excited about your faith? And do you make your enthusiasm known to those around you? Or are you a "silent ambassador" for Christ? God's preference is clear: He intends that you stand before others and talk about your faith. So today, make sure to share your faith and your excitement. The world needs both.

As you walk by faith, you live a righteous life, for righteousness is always by faith.

Kay Arthur

Abandoning the Status Quo

I have come as a light into the world, so that everyone who believes in Me would not remain in darkness.

—John 12:46 Holman CSB

Okay, answer this question honestly: Do you behave differently because of your relationship with Jesus? Or do you behave in pretty much the same way that you would if you weren't a believer? Hopefully, the fact that you've invited Christ to reign over your heart means that you've made BIG changes in your thoughts and your actions.

Doing the right thing is not always easy, especially when you're tired or frustrated. But, doing the wrong thing almost always leads to trouble. And sometimes, it leads to big trouble.

If you're determined to follow "the crowd," you may soon find yourself headed in the wrong direction. So here's some advice: Don't follow the crowd—follow Jesus. And keep following Him every day of your life.

The measure of a man is not what he does on Sunday, but rather who he is Monday through Saturday.

Anonymous

Barnabas,
the Encouraging Friend

Now Joseph, a Levite of Cyprian birth, who was also called Barnabas by the apostles (which translated means Son of Encouragement)…

—Acts 4:36 NASB

Barnabas, a man whose name meant "Son of Encouragement," was a leader in the early Christian church. He was known for his kindness and for his ability to encourage others. Because of Barnabas, many people were introduced to Christ. And today, as believers living in a difficult world, we must seek to imitate the "Son of Encouragement."

We imitate Barnabas when we speak kind words to our families and to our friends. We imitate Barnabas when our actions give credence to our beliefs. We imitate Barnabas when we are generous with our possessions and with our praise. We imitate Barnabas when we give hope to the hopeless and encouragement to the downtrodden.

Today, be like Barnabas: become a source of encouragement to those who cross your path. When you do so, you will quite literally change the world, one person—and one moment—at a time.

Be Careful!

Be careful! Watch out for attacks from the Devil, your great enemy. He prowls around like a roaring lion, looking for some victim to devour. Take a firm stand against him, and be strong in your faith.

—1 Peter 5:8-9 NLT

If you stop to think about it, the cold, hard evidence is right in front of your eyes: you live in a temptation-filled world. The devil is out on the street, hard at work, causing pain and heartache in more ways than ever before. Yep, you live in a temptation nation, a place where the bad guys are working 24/7 to lead you astray. That's why you must remain vigilant. Not only must you resist Satan when he confronts you, but you must also avoid those places where Satan can most easily tempt you.

In a letter to believers, Peter offers a stern warning: "Your adversary, the devil, prowls around like a roaring lion, seeking someone to devour" (I Peter 5:8 NASB). What was true in New Testament times is equally true in our own. Satan tempts his prey and then devours them (and it's up to you—and only you—to make sure that you're not one of the ones being devoured!). Satan is determined to win; we must be equally determined that he does not.

Because Christ has faced
our every temptation without sin,
we never face a temptation that
has no door of escape.

—

Beth Moore

Choosing Wisely

I am offering you life or death, blessings or curses. Now, choose life! . . . To choose life is to love the Lord your God, obey him, and stay close to him.

—Deuteronomy 30:19-20 NCV

Choices, choices, choices! You've got so many choices to make, and sometimes, making those choices isn't easy. At times you're torn between what you want to do and what you ought to do. When that happens, it's up to you to choose wisely . . . or else!

When you make wise choices, you are rewarded; when you make unwise choices, you must accept the consequences. It's as simple as that. So make sure that your choices are pleasing to God . . . or else!

No matter how many books you read, no matter how many schools you attend, you're never really wise until you start making wise choices.

Marie T. Freeman

You have to say "yes" to God first before you can effectively say "no" to the devil.

Vance Havner

Safety Matters

The prudent see danger and take refuge, but the simple keep going and suffer from it.

—Proverbs 27:12 NIV

Self-control and safety go hand in hand. Why? Because a big part of self-control is looking around and thinking things through before you do something that you might regret later.

Remember the saying "Look before you leap!"? Well, if you want to live safely and happily, you should look very carefully before you decide whether or not to leap. After all, it's easy to leap, but once you're in the middle of your jump, it's too late to leap back!

God's plan for our guidance is for us to grow gradually in wisdom before we get to the crossroads.

Bill Hybels

The essence of wisdom, from a practical standpoint, is pausing long enough to look at our lives—invitations, opportunities, relationships—from God's perspective. And then acting on it.

Charles Stanley

Guided by Honesty

Good people will be guided by honesty; dishonesty will destroy those who are not trustworthy.

—Proverbs 11:3 NCV

Charles Swindoll observed, "Nothing speaks louder or more powerfully than a life of integrity." And, of course, he was right!

Integrity is built slowly over a lifetime. It is a precious thing—difficult to build but easy to tear down. As believers in Christ, we must seek to live each day with discipline, honesty, and faith. When we do, at least two things happen: integrity becomes a habit, and God blesses us because of our obedience to Him.

Living a life of integrity isn't always the easiest way, but it is always right way. And God clearly intends that it should be our way, too.

God never called us to naïveté. He called us to integrity.... The biblical concept of integrity emphasizes mature innocence not childlike ignorance.

Beth Moore

Since Tomorrow Is Not Promised

We must do the works of Him who sent Me while it is day. Night is coming when no one can work.

—John 9:4 Holman CSB

The words of John 9:4 remind us that "night is coming" for all of us. But until then, God gives us each day and fills it to the brim with possibilities. The day is presented to us fresh and clean at midnight, free of charge, but we must beware: Today is a non-renewable resource—once it's gone, it's gone forever. Our responsibility, of course, is to use this day in the service of God's will and in accordance with His commandments.

Today, treasure the time that God has given you. And search for the hidden possibilities that God has placed along your path. This day is a priceless gift from your Creator, so use it joyfully and productively. And encourage others to do likewise. After all, night is coming when no one can work . . .

Today is a gift from God. That's why it is called "The Present."

Anonymous

The Rich Harvest

Now this I say, he who sows sparingly will also reap sparingly, and he who sows bountifully will also reap bountifully.

—2 Corinthians 9:6 NASB

How can we serve God? By sharing His message and His love with those who cross our paths.

Everywhere we look, or so it seems, the needs are great. And at every turn, it seems, so are the temptations. Still, our challenge is clear: we must love God, obey His commandments, trust His Son, and serve His children. When we place the Lord in His rightful place—at the center of our lives—we will reap a bountiful spiritual harvest that will endure forever.

That's what I love about serving God. In His eyes, there are no little people . . . because there are no big people. We are all on the same playing field.

Joni Eareckson Tada

Service is the pathway to real significance.

Rick Warren

Jesus Gives Life

For whoever finds me finds life and receives favor from the LORD.

—Proverbs 8:35 NIV

Who's the best friend this world has ever had? Jesus, of course! When you invite Him into your heart, Jesus will be your friend, too . . . your friend forever.

Jesus has offered to share the gifts of everlasting life and everlasting love with the world . . . and with you. If you make mistakes, He'll still be your friend. If you behave badly, He'll still love you. If you feel sorry or sad, He can help you feel better.

Jesus wants you to have a happy, healthy life. He wants you to be generous and kind. He wants you to follow His example. And the rest is up to you. You can do it! And with a friend like Jesus, you will.

There is not a single thing that Jesus cannot change, control, and conquer because He is the living Lord.

Franklin Graham

Trusting God's Love

Do you think anyone is going to be able to drive a wedge between us and Christ's love for us? There is no way! Not trouble, not hard times, not hatred, not hunger, not homelessness, not bullying threats, not backstabbing, not even the worst sins listed in Scripture…I'm absolutely convinced that nothing, nothing living or dead, angelic or demonic, today or tomorrow, high or low, thinkable or unthinkable, absolutely nothing can get between us and God's love because of the way that Jesus our Master has embraced us.

—Romans 8:35, 38-39 MSG

The Bible makes it clear: God's got a plan—a very big plan—and you're an important part of that plan. But here's the catch: God won't force His plans upon you; you've got to figure things out for yourself.

As a follower of Christ, you should ask yourself this question: "How closely can I make my plans match God's plans?" The more closely you manage to follow the path that God intends for your life, the better.

Do you have hopes and expectations? Talk to God about your dreams. Are you carefully planning for the days and weeks ahead? Consult God as you establish your priorities. Turn every concern over to your Heavenly Father, and sincerely seek His guidance—prayerfully, earnestly, and often. Then, listen for His answers . . . and trust the answers that He gives.

Rejoice!

My purpose is to give life in all its fullness.

—John 10:10 HSCB

Have you made the choice to rejoice? Hopefully so. After all, if you're a believer, you have plenty of reasons to be joyful. Yet sometimes, amid the inevitable hustle and bustle of life here on earth, you may lose sight of your blessings as you wrestle with the challenges of everyday life.

Christ made it clear to His followers: He intended that His joy would become their joy. And it still holds true today: Christ intends that His believers share His love with His joy in their hearts.

What does life have in store for you? A world full of possibilities (of course it's up to you to seize them), and God's promise of abundance (of course it's up to you to accept it). So, as you embark upon the next phase of your journey, remember to celebrate the life that God has given you. Your Creator has blessed you beyond measure. Honor Him with your prayers, your words, your deeds, and your joy.

God's riches are beyond anything we could ask or even dare to imagine! If my life gets gooey and stale, I have no excuse.

Barbara Johnson

The Golden Rule

Here is a simple, rule-of-thumb for behavior: Ask yourself what you want people to do for you, then grab the initiative and do it for them. Add up God's Law and Prophets and this is what you get.

—Matthew 7:12 MSG

Would you like to make the world a better place? If so, you can start by practicing the Golden Rule.

Jesus said, "Do to others what you want them to do to you" (Matthew 7:12 NCV). That means that you should treat other people in the very same way that you want to be treated. That's the Golden Rule.

Is the Golden Rule your rule, or is it just another Bible verse that goes in one ear and out the other? Jesus made Himself perfectly clear: He instructed you to treat other people in the same way that you want to be treated. But sometimes, especially when you're feeling pressure from friends, or when you're tired or upset, obeying the Golden Rule can seem like an impossible task—but it's not. So if you want to know how to treat other people, ask the person you see every time you look into the mirror. The answer you receive will tell you exactly what to do.

He's Listening

One day Jesus told his disciples a story to illustrate their need for constant prayer and to show them that they must never give up.

—Luke 18:1 NLT

Are you faced with a difficult choice or an important decision? Then pray about it. If you talk to God sincerely and often, He won't lead you astray. Instead, God will guide you and help you make more intelligent choices . . . if you take the time to talk with Him.

If you have questions about whether you should do something or not, pray about it. If there is something you're worried about, ask God to comfort you. If you're having trouble with your relationships, ask God to help you sort things out. As you pray more, you'll discover that God is always near and that He's always ready to hear from you. So don't worry about things; pray about them. God is waiting . . . and listening!

What God gives in answer to our prayers will always be the thing we most urgently need, and it will always be sufficient.

Elisabeth Elliot

Each Day Is a Gift

How happy are those who can live in your house, always singing your praises. How happy are those who are strong in the Lord....

—Psalm 84:4-5 NLT

God wants you to have a happy, joyful life. But that doesn't mean that you'll be happy all the time. Sometimes, you won't feel like feeling happy, and when you don't, your attitude won't be very good.

When you're feeling a little tired or sad, here's something to remember: This day is a gift from God. And it's up to you to enjoy this day by trying to be cheerful, helpful, courteous, and well behaved. How can you do these things? A good place to start is by doing your best to think good thoughts.

When we do what is right, we have contentment, peace, and happiness.

Beverly LaHaye

Perfect obedience would be perfect happiness, if only we had perfect confidence in the power we were obeying.

Corrie ten Boom

Giving God
Your Complete Attention

Worship the Lord your God and . . . serve Him only.

—Matthew 4:10 Holman CSB

Ninteenth-century clergyman Edwin Hubbel Chapin warned, "Neutral people are the devil's allies." His words were true then, and they're true now. Apathy in the face of evil is a sin. Yet all too often, we fail to fight evil, not because we are apathetic, but because we are shortsighted: we don't fight the devil because we don't recognize his handiwork.

If we are to recognize evil and fight it, we must pay careful attention. We must pay attention to God's Word, and we must pay attention to the realities of everyday life. When we look at life with eyes and hearts that are attuned to God's Word, we can no longer be neutral Christians. And when we are no longer neutral, God rejoices while the devil despairs.

The greatest enemy of holiness is not passion; it is apathy.

John Eldredge

Finding Purpose Through Charity

Happy is the person who thinks about the poor. When trouble comes, the Lord will save him.

—Psalm 41:1 NCV

God's Words commands us to be generous, compassionate servants to those who need our help. As believers, we have been richly blessed by our Creator. We, in turn, are called to share our gifts, our possessions, and our talents.

Corrie ten Boom correctly observed, "The measure of a life is not its duration but its donation." These words remind us that the quality of our lives is determined not by what we are able to take from others, but instead by what we are able to share with others.

The thread of generosity is woven into the very fabric of Christ's teachings. If we are to be His disciples, then we, too, must be cheerful, generous, courageous givers. Our Savior expects no less from us. And He deserves no less.

The measure of a life, after all, is not its duration but its donation.

Corrie ten Boom

God's Greatest Promise

I assure you: Anyone who believes has eternal life.

—John 6:47 Holman CSB

It's time to remind yourself of a promise that God made a long time ago—the promise that God sent His Son Jesus to save the world and to save you! And when you stop to think about it, there can be no greater promise than that.

No matter where you are, God is with you. God loves you, and He sent His Son so that you can live forever in heaven with your loved ones. WOW! That's the greatest promise in the history of the universe. The End.

God has promised us abundance, peace, and eternal life. These treasures are ours for the asking; all we must do is claim them. One of the great mysteries of life is why on earth do so many of us wait so very long to lay claim to God's gifts?

Marie T. Freeman

And because we know Christ is alive, we have hope for the present and hope for life beyond the grave.

Billy Graham

Friends You Can Trust

Friends come and friends go, but a true friend sticks by you like family.

—Proverbs 18:24 MSG

All lasting friendships are built upon both honesty and trust. Without trust, friends soon drift apart. But with trust, friends can stay friends for a lifetime.

As Christians, we should always try to be trustworthy friends. And, we should be thankful for the people who are loyal friends to us. When we treat other people with honesty and respect, we not only make more friends, but we also keep the friendships we've already made.

Do you want friends you can trust? Then start by being a friend they can trust. That's the way to make your friendships strong, stronger, and strongest!

True friends don't spend time gazing into each other's eyes. They show great tenderness toward each other, but they face in the same direction, toward common projects, interest, goals, and above all, toward a common Lord.

C. S. Lewis

The Way We Treat
Our Neighbors

*The whole law is made complete in this one command: "Love
your neighbor as you love yourself."*

—Galatians 5:14 NCV

How should we treat other people? God's Word is
clear: we should treat others in the same way that we wish
to be treated. This Golden Rule is easy to understand, but
sometimes it can be difficult to live by.

Because we are imperfect human beings, we are, on
occasion, selfish, thoughtless, or cruel. But God commands
us to behave otherwise. He teaches us to rise above our
own imperfections and to treat others with unselfishness
and love. When we observe God's Golden Rule, we help
build His kingdom here on earth. And, when we share the
love of Christ, we share a priceless gift; may we share it
today and every day that we live.

If my heart is right with God, every human being is my
neighbor.

Oswald Chambers

God Wrote a Book

For I am not ashamed of the gospel, because it is God's power for salvation to everyone who believes.

—Romans 1:16 Holman CSB

If you want to know God, you should read the book He wrote. It's called the Bible (of course!), and God uses it to teach you and guide you. The Bible is not like any other book. It is an amazing gift from your Heavenly Father.

D. L. Moody observed, "The Bible was not given to increase our knowledge but to change our lives." God's Holy Word is, indeed, a life-changing, one-of-a-kind treasure. Handle it with care, but more importantly, handle it every day!

Daily Bible reading is essential to victorious living and real Christian growth.

Billy Graham

Study the Bible and observe how the persons behaved and how God dealt with them. There is explicit teaching on every condition of life.

Corrie ten Boom

Your Roadmap

Teach me, O Lord, the way of Your statutes, and I shall keep it to the end.

—Psalm 119:33 NKJV

As you look to the future and decide upon the direction of your life, what will you use as your roadmap? Will you trust God's Holy Word and use it as an indispensable tool to guide your steps? Or will you choose a different map to guide your steps? The map you choose will determine the quality of your journey and its ultimate destination.

The Bible is the ultimate guide for life; make it your guidebook as well. When you do, you can be comforted in the knowledge that your steps are guided by a Source of wisdom and truth that never fails.

The Bible was not given to increase our knowledge but to change our lives.

D. L. Moody

Faith isn't the ability to believe long and far into the misty future. It's simply taking God at His word and taking the next step.

Joni Eareckson Tada

Using Time Wisely

Teach us to number our days carefully so that we may develop wisdom in our hearts.

—Psalm 90:12 Holman CSB

An important element of our service to God is the way that we choose to spend the time He has entrusted to us. Each waking moment holds the potential to do a good deed, to say a kind word, or to offer a heartfelt prayer. Our challenge, as Christians, is use our time wisely in the service of God's work and in accordance with His plan for our lives.

Each day is a special treasure to be savored and celebrated. May we—as Christians who have so much to celebrate—never fail to praise our Creator by rejoicing in this glorious day, and by using it wisely.

God has a present will for your life. It is neither chaotic nor utterly exhausting. In the midst of many good choices vying for your time, He will give you the discernment to recognize what is best.

Beth Moore

A God of Possibilities

But Jesus looked at them and said, "With men this is impossible, but with God all things are possible."

—Matthew 19:26 Holman CSB

If you really want to know God, you must be willing to worship Him seven days a week, not just on Sunday.

God has a wonderful plan for your life, and an important part of that plan includes the time that you set aside for praise and worship. Every life, including yours, is based upon some form of worship. The question is not whether you will worship, but what you worship.

If you choose to worship God, you will receive a king-sized harvest of blessings. But if you distance yourself from God, you're making a huge mistake. So do this: Worship God today and every day. Worship Him with sincerity and thanksgiving. Write His name on your heart and rest assured that He, too, has written your name on His.

When offered without a sincere heart, every form of worship is a mockery.

C. H. Spurgeon

Persistent Prayer

Watch therefore, and pray always. . . .

—Luke 21:36 NKJV

When we weave the habit of prayer into the very fabric of our days, we invite God to become a partner in every aspect of our lives. When we consult God on an hourly basis, we avail ourselves of His wisdom, His strength, and His love. Today, instead of turning things over in your mind, turn them over to God in prayer. Instead of worrying about your next decision, decide to let God lead the way. Don't limit your prayers to meals or to bedtime. Pray constantly about things great and small. God is listening, and He wants to hear from you. Now.

I learned as never before that persistent calling upon the Lord breaks through every stronghold of the devil, for nothing is impossible with God. For Christians in these troubled times, there is simply no other way.

Jim Cymbala

Prayerful Hearts and Willing Hands

So you may walk in the way of goodness, and keep to the paths of righteousness. For the upright will dwell in the land, And the blameless will remain in it.

—Proverbs 2:20-21 NKJV

The old adage is both familiar and true: We must pray as if everything depended upon God, but work as if everything depended upon us. Yet sometimes, when we are tired or discouraged, we may allow our worries to sap our energy and our hope. God has other intentions. God intends that we pray for things, and He intends that we be willing to work for the things that we pray for. More importantly, God intends that our work should become His work.

If you have concerns about the inevitable challenges of everyday living, take those concerns to God in prayer. He will guide your steps, He will calm your fears, and He will reward your efforts.

Great relief and satisfaction can come from seeking God's priorities for us in each season, discerning what is "best" in the midst of many noble opportunities, and pouring our most excellent energies into those things.

Beth Moore

Quiet Charity

Be careful not to do your acts of righteousness before men, to be seen by them. If you do, you will have no reward from your Father in heaven.

—Matthew 6:1 NIV

Hymn writer Fanny Crosby wrote, "To God be the glory; great thing He hath done!" But sometimes, because we are imperfect human beings, we seek the glory. Sometimes, when we do good deeds, we seek to glorify our achievements in a vain attempt build ourselves up in the eyes of our neighbors. To do so is a profound mistake.

God's Word gives specific instructions about how we should approach our acts of charity: The glory must go to God, not to us. All praise belongs to the Giver of all good gifts: our Father in Heaven. We are simply conduits for His generosity, and we must remain humble . . . extremely humble.

We can't do everything, but can we do anything more valuable than invest ourselves in another?

Elisabeth Elliot

Today's Happiness

But happy are those . . . whose hope is in the LORD their God.
—Psalm 146:5 NLT

If we could decide to be happy "once and for all," life would be so much simpler, but it doesn't seem to work that way. If we want happiness to last, we need to create good thoughts every day that we live. Yesterday's good thoughts don't count . . . we've got to think more good thoughts today.

Each new day is a gift from God, so treat it that way. Think about it like this: today is another wonderful chance to celebrate God's gifts.

So celebrate—starting now—and keep celebrating forever!

Father and Mother lived on the edge of poverty, and yet their contentment was not dependent upon their surroundings. Their relationship to each other and to the Lord gave them strength and happiness.

Corrie ten Boom

The Bible says that being a Christian is not only a great way to die, but it's also the best way to live.

Bill Hybels

The Search for Wisdom

If you don't know what you're doing, pray to the Father. He loves to help. You'll get his help, and won't be condescended to when you ask for it. Ask boldly, believingly, without a second thought. People who "worry their prayers" are like wind-whipped waves. Don't think you're going to get anything from the Master that way, adrift at sea, keeping all your options open.

—James 1:5-8 MSG

Do you seek the wisdom that only God can give? If so, ask Him for it! If you ask God for guidance, He will not withhold it. If you petition Him sincerely, and if you genuinely seek to form a relationship with Him, your Heavenly Father will guide your steps and enlighten your heart. But be forewarned: You will not acquire God's wisdom without obeying His commandments. Why? Because God's wisdom is more than just a collection of thoughts; it is, first and foremost, a way of life.

Wisdom is as wisdom does. So if you sincerely seek God's wisdom, don't be satisfied to learn something; make up your mind to become something. And then, as you allow God to remake you in the image of His Son, you will most surely become wise.

The Source of Strength

Happy are the people whose strength is in You, whose hearts are set on pilgrimage.

—Psalm 84:5 Holman CSB

Have you "tapped in" to the power of God? Have you turned your life and your heart over to Him, or are you muddling along under your own power? The answer to this question will determine the quality of your life here on earth and the destiny of your life throughout all eternity.

The Bible tells us that we can do all things through the power of our risen Savior, Jesus Christ. But what does the Bible say about our powers outside the will of Christ? The Bible teaches us that "the wages of sin is death" (Romans 6:23). Our challenge, then, is clear: we must place Christ where He belongs: at the very center of our lives. When we do so, we will surely discover that He offers us the strength to live victoriously in this world and eternally in the next.

Because He lives, I can face tomorrow; because He lives, all fear is gone; because I know He holds the future, and life is worth the living just because He lives.

Gloria Gaither and William J. Gaither

The Search for Truth

You will know the truth, and the truth will set you free.

—John 8:32 Holman CSB

The words of John 8:32 are both familiar and profound: the truth, indeed, will make you free. Truth is God's way: He commands His children to live in truth, and He rewards those who follow His commandment. Jesus is the personification of a perfect, liberating truth that offers salvation to mankind.

Do you seek to walk with God? Do you seek to feel God's peace? Then you must walk in truth, and you must walk with the Savior. There is simply no other way.

I would rather know the truth than be happy in ignorance. If I cannot have both truth and happiness, give me truth. We'll have a long time to be happy in heaven.

A. W. Tozer

The Holy Spirit was given to guide us into all truth, but He doesn't do it all at once.

Elisabeth Elliot

Encouraging Words for Family and Friends

Good people's words will help many others.

—Proverbs 10:21 NCV

Life is a team sport, and all of us need occasional pats on the back from our teammates. As Christians, we are called upon to spread the Good News of Christ, and we are also called to spread a message of encouragement and hope to the world.

Whether you realize it or not, many people with whom you come in contact every day are in desperate need of a smile or an encouraging word. The world can be a difficult place, and countless friends and family members may be troubled by the challenges of everyday life. Since you don't always know who needs your help, the best strategy is to try to encourage all the people who cross your path. So today, be a world-class source of encouragement to everyone you meet. Never has the need been greater.

Sometimes one little spark of kindness is all it takes to reignite the light of hope in a heart that's blinded by pain.

Barbara Johnson

When People Are Cruel

A kind man benefits himself, but a cruel man brings disaster on himself.

—Proverbs 11:17 Holman CSB

Face it: sometimes people can be cruel. And when people are unkind to you or to your friends, you may be tempted to strike back in anger. Don't do it! Instead, remember that God corrects other people's behaviors in His own way, and He doesn't need your help. So even when other people misbehave, God wants you to forgive them . . . and that's what you should do.

There's a lot in the world we ought to be very angry about: oppression, injustice, discrimination, and cruelty that mistreats the poor and makes fun of the disabled.

Bill Hybels

We are in a continual battle with the spiritual forces of evil, but we will triumph when we yield to God's leading and call on His powerful presence in prayer.

Shirley Dobson

Keeping Up Appearances

Man does not see what the Lord sees, for man sees what is visible, but the Lord sees the heart.

—1 Samuel 16:7 Holman CSB

The world sees you as you appear to be; God sees you as you really are. He sees your heart, and He understands your intentions. The opinions of others should be relatively unimportant to you; however, God's view of you—His understanding of your actions, your thoughts, and your motivations—should be vitally important.

Few things in life are more futile than "keeping up appearances" in order to impress your friends and your dates—yet the media would have you believe otherwise. The media would have you believe that everything depends on the color of your hair, the condition of your wardrobe, and the model of the car you drive. But nothing could be further from the truth. What is important, of course, is pleasing your Father in heaven. You please Him when your intentions are pure and your actions are just. When you do, you will be blessed today, tomorrow, and forever.

It is comfortable to know that we are responsible to God and not to man. It is a small matter to be judged of man's judgement.

Lottie Moon

The Wisdom of Righteousness

As shameful conduct is pleasure for a fool, so wisdom is for a man of understanding.

—Proverbs 10:23 Holman CSB

Are you a radically different girl because of your decision to form a personal relationship with Jesus? Has Jesus made a BIG difference in your life, or are you basically the same person you were before you invited Him into your heart? The answer to these questions will determine the quality and the direction of your life.

If you're still doing all the same things you did before you became a Christian, it may be time to take an honest look at the current condition of your faith. Why? Because Jesus doesn't want you to be a run-of-the-mill, follow-the-crowd kind of girl. Jesus wants you to be a "new creation" through Him. And that's exactly what you should want for yourself, too.

Although God causes all things to work together for good for His children, He still holds us accountable for our behavior.

Kay Arthur

Happy Thoughts

Those who are pure in their thinking are happy, because they will be with God.

—Matthew 5:8 NCV

Do you try to think the kind of thoughts that make you happy, not sad? The Bible says that you should. Do you try to think about things that are true and right? The Bible says that you should.

Do you turn away from bad thoughts—and away from people who misbehave? The Bible says that you should.

The Bible instructs you to guard your thoughts against things that are hurtful or wrong. So remember this: when you turn away from the bad thoughts, you've made a very wise choice.

The moment anxious thoughts invade your mind, go to the Lord in prayer. Look first to God. Then, you will see the cause of your anxiety in a whole new light.

Kay Arthur

Preoccupy my thoughts with your praise beginning today.

Joni Eareckson Tada

Moving On

Bad temper is contagious—don't get infected.

—Proverbs 22:25 MSG

Today and every day, make sure that you're a person who is known for the kind way that you treat everybody. That's how God wants you to behave.

And if someone says something to you that isn't very nice, don't pay too much attention. Just forgive that person as quickly as you can, and try to move on . . . as quickly as you can.

We are all fallen creatures and all very hard to live with.

C. S. Lewis

By not forgiving, by not letting wrongs go, we aren't getting back at anyone. We are merely punishing ourselves by barricading our own hearts.

Jim Cymbala

Bitterness is the trap that snares the hunter.

Max Lucado

Don't Fall in Love with Worldy Things

Don't love the world's ways. Don't love the world's goods. Love of the world squeezes out love for the Father. Practically everything that goes on in the world—wanting your own way, wanting everything for yourself, wanting to appear important—has nothing to do with the Father. It just isolates you from him. The world and all its wanting, wanting, wanting is on the way out—but whoever does what God wants is set for eternity.

—1 John 2:15-17 MSG

We live in the world, but we should not worship it. Our job is to place God first and everything else second. But sometimes, putting God in His rightful place is often difficult. In fact, at every turn, or so it seems, we are tempted to do otherwise.

The 21st-century world is a noisy, distracting place filled with countless opportunities to stray from God's will. The world seems to cry, "Worship me with your time, your money, your energy, and your thoughts!" But God commands otherwise: He commands us to worship Him and Him alone; everything else must be secondary.

Our joy ends where love of the world begins.

C. H. Spurgeon

Lessons in Patience

Give all your worries and cares to God, for he cares about what happens to you.

—1 Peter 5:6 NLT

Are you anxious for God to work out His plan for your life? Who isn't? As believers, we all want God to do great things for us and through us, and we want Him to do those things now. But sometimes, God has other plans. Sometimes, God's timetable does not coincide with our own. It's worth noting, however, that God's timetable is always perfect.

The next time you find your patience tested to the limit, remember that the world unfolds according to God's plan, not ours. Sometimes, we must wait patiently, and that's as it should be. After all, think how patient God has been with us.

To wait upon God is the perfection of activity.

Oswald Chambers

Waiting on God brings us to the journey's end quicker than our feet.

Mrs. Charles E. Cowman

According to God

The counsel of the LORD stands forever, the plans of His heart from generation to generation.

—Psalm 33:11 NASB

God's wisdom stands forever. God's Word is a light for every generation. Make it your light as well. Use the Bible as a compass for the next stage of your life's journey. Use it as the yardstick by which your behavior is measured. And as you carefully consult the pages of God's Word, prayerfully ask Him to reveal the wisdom that you need. When you take your concerns to God, He will not turn you away; He will, instead, offer answers that are tested and true. Your job is to ask, to listen, and to trust.

We can always gauge where we are by the teachings of Jesus Christ.

Oswald Chambers

Train your child in the way in which you know you should have gone yourself.

C. H. Spurgeon

Demonstrating Your Faith

So brothers and sisters, be careful that none of you has an evil, unbelieving heart that will turn you away from the living God. But encourage each other every day while it is "today." Help each other so none of you will become hardened because sin has tricked you.

—Hebrews 3:13 NCV

Let's face facts: those of us who are Christians should be willing to talk about the things that Christ has done for us. Our personal stories are vitally important, but sometimes, because of shyness or insecurities, we're afraid to share our experiences. And that's unfortunate.

We live in a world that desperately needs the healing message of Christ Jesus. Every believer, each in his or her own way, bears responsibility for sharing the Good News of our Savior. And it is important to remember that we bear testimony through both words and actions.

If you seek to be a radical follower of Christ, then it's time for you to share your testimony with others. So today, preach the Gospel through your words and your deeds… but not necessarily in that order.

Your light is the truth of the Gospel message itself as well as your witness as to Who Jesus is and what He has done for you. Don't hide it.

Anne Graham Lotz

The Person in the Mirror

For you made us only a little lower than God, and you crowned us with glory and honor.

—Psalm 8:5 NLT

Do you really like the person you see when you look into the mirror? You should! After all, the person in the mirror is a very special person who is made—and loved—by God.

In fact, you are loved in many, many ways: God loves you, your parents love you, and your family loves you, for starters. So you should love yourself, too.

So here's something to think about: since God thinks you're special, and since so many people think you're special, isn't it about time for you to agree with them? Of course it is! It's time to say, "You're very wonderful and very special," to the person you see in the mirror.

God specializes in things fresh and firsthand. His plans for you this year may outshine those of the past. He's prepared to fill your days with reasons to give Him praise.

Joni Eareckson Tada

If You Think You Can

Though a righteous man falls seven times, he will get up, but the wicked will stumble into ruin.

—Proverbs 24:16 Holman CSB

If you think you can do something, then you can probably do it. If you think you can't do something, then you probably won't do it.

So remember this: if you're having a little trouble getting something done, don't get mad, don't get frustrated, don't get discouraged, and don't give up. Just keep trying . . . and believe in yourself.

When you try hard—and keep trying hard—you can really do amazing things . . . but if you quit at the first sign of trouble, you'll miss out. So here's a good rule to follow: when you have something that you want to finish, finish it . . . and finish it sooner rather than later.

We don't give up. We look up. We trust. We believe. And our optimism is not hollow. Christ has proven worthy. He has shown that he never fails. That's what makes God, God.

Max Lucado

Every Moment Matters

Lord, tell me when the end will come and how long I will live. Let me know how long I have. You have given me only a short life . . . . Everyone's life is only a breath.

—Psalm 39:4–5 NCV

Every day, like every life, is composed of moments. Each moment of your life holds within it the potential to seek God's will and to serve His purposes. If you are wise, you will try to do both.

An important part of wisdom is the wise use of time. How will you invest your time today? Will you savor the moments of your life, or will you squander them? Will you use your time as an instrument of God's will, or will you allow commonplace distractions to rule your day and your life?

The gift of time is a gift from God. Treat it as if it were a precious, fleeting, one-of-a-kind treasure. Because it is.

Frustration is not the will of God. There is time to do anything and everything that God wants us to do.

Elisabeth Elliot

Making the Most of Our Talents

Do not neglect the spiritual gift that is within you....
—1 Timothy 4:14 NASB

Face it: you've got a collection of talents that need to be improved. All people possess special gifts—bestowed from the Father above—and you are no exception. But, your gift is no guarantee of success; it must be cultivated—by you—or it will go unused . . . and God's gift to you will be squandered.

Today, make a promise to yourself that you will earnestly seek to discover the talents that God has given you. Then, nourish those talents and make them grow. Finally, vow to share your gifts with the world for as long as God gives you the power to do so. After all, the best way to say "Thank You" for God's gifts is to use them.

You are the only person on earth who can use your ability.

Zig Ziglar

Words Worthy of Our Savior

When you talk, do not say harmful things, but say what people need—words that will help others become stronger. Then what you say will do good to those who listen to you.

—Ephesians 4:29 NCV

Are you a person who consistently uses words that are pleasing to God? Hopefully so. If you genuinely desire to be a good person, your words and your actions must demonstrate your faithfulness to the Creator.

Of course you must never take the Lord's name in vain, but it doesn't stop there. You must also try to speak words of encouragement, words that lift others up, words that give honor to your Heavenly Father.

The Bible clearly warns that you will be judged by the words you speak, so choose those words carefully. And remember this: God is always listening.

Fill the heart with the love of Christ so that only truth and purity can come out of the mouth.

Warren Wiersbe

The Right Path

Now that you are obedient children of God do not live as you did in the past. You did not understand, so you did the evil things you wanted. But be holy in all you do, just as God, the One who called you, is holy.

—1 Peter 1:14-15 NCV

How will you respond to Christ's love? Will you take up His cross and follow Him, or will you choose another path? When you place your hopes squarely at the foot of the cross, when you place Jesus squarely at the center of your life, you will be blessed.

The 19th-century writer Hannah Whitall Smith observed, "The crucial question for each of us is this: What do you think of Jesus, and do you yet have a personal acquaintance with Him?" Indeed, the answer to that question determines the quality, the course, and the direction of our lives today and for all eternity.

Let us put down our old ways and pick up His cross. Let us walk the path that He walked.

Holiness should be a constant goal for all of us. Christ prepares us for the perfection of heaven by lessening the imperfections of earth.

Shirley Dobson

Lifetime Learning

Above all and before all, do this: Get Wisdom! Write this at the top of your list: Get Understanding!

—Proverbs 4:7 MSG

God has lessons He wants to teach all of us. And, of course, the best way to learn these lessons is to learn them the first time God tries to teach us. Unfortunately, too many of us learn much more slowly than that.

When we resist God's instruction, He continues to teach, whether we like it or not. And if we keep making the same old mistakes, God responds by rewarding us with the same old results.

Our challenge, then, is to discern God's lessons from the experiences of everyday life. Hopefully, we learn those lessons sooner rather than later because the sooner we do, the sooner He can move on to the next lesson and the next, and the next . . .

It seems to me that happiness is not the major goal of life, but instead is a wonderful by-product.

Warren Wiersbe

Habits That Are Pleasing to God

I, the Lord, examine the mind, I test the heart to give to each according to his way, according to what his actions deserve.

—Jeremiah 17:10 Holman CSB

It's an old saying and a true one: First, you make your habits, and then your habits make you. Some habits will inevitably bring you closer to God; other habits will lead you away from the path He has chosen for you. If you sincerely desire to improve your spiritual health, you must honestly examine the habits that make up the fabric of your day. And you must abandon those habits that are displeasing to God.

If you trust God, and if you keep asking for His help, He can transform your life. If you sincerely ask Him to help you, the same God who created the universe will help you defeat the harmful habits that have heretofore defeated you. So, if at first you don't succeed, keep praying. God is listening, and He's ready to help you become a better person if you ask Him . . . so ask today.

You can build up a set of good habits so that you habitually take the Christian way without thought.

E. Stanley Jones

Prayer is a habit.
Worship is a habit.
Kindness is a habit.
And if you want to please God,
you'd better make sure that these
habits are your habits.

—

Marie T. Freeman

Following His Footsteps

But whoever keeps His word, truly in him the love of God is perfected. This is how we know we are in Him: the one who says he remains in Him should walk just as He walked.

—1 John 2:5-6 Holman CSB

Life is a series of decisions and choices. Each day, we make countless decisions that can bring us closer to God... or not. Do you seek to walk in the footsteps of the One from Galilee, or will you choose another path? If you sincerely seek God's peace and His blessings, then you must strive to imitate God's Son.

Thomas Brooks spoke for believers of every generation when he observed, "Christ is the sun, and all the watches of our lives should be set by the dial of his motion." Christ, indeed, is the ultimate Savior of mankind and the personal Savior of those who believe in Him. As His servants, we should walk in His footsteps as we share His love and His message with a world that needs both.

Think of this—we may live together with Him here and now, a daily walking with Him who loved us and gave Himself for us.

Elisabeth Elliot

Aiming High

I can do everything through him that gives me strength.

—Philippians 4:13 NIV

Are you willing to dream big dreams? Hopefully so; after all, God promises that we can do "all things" through Him. Yet most of us, even the most devout among us, live far below our potential. We take half measures; we dream small dreams; we waste precious time and energy on the distractions of the world. But God has other plans for us. Our Creator intends that we live faithfully, hopefully, courageously, and abundantly. He knows that we are capable of so much more; and He wants us to do the things we're capable of doing; and He wants us to start doing those things now.

You cannot out-dream God.

John Eldredge

Allow your dreams a place in your prayers and plans. God-given dreams can help you move into the future He is preparing for you.

Barbara Johnson

The Goal Is to Please God

Our only goal is to please God whether we live here or there, because we must all stand before Christ to be judged.

—2 Corinthians 5:9-10 NCV

Rick Warren observed, "Those who follow the crowd usually get lost in it." We know those words to be true, but oftentimes we fail to live by them. Instead of trusting God for guidance, we imitate our friends and suffer the consequences. Instead of seeking to please our Father in heaven, we strive to please our peers, with decidedly mixed results. Instead of doing the right thing, we do the "easy" thing or the "popular" thing. And when we do, we pay a high price for our shortsightedness.

Would you like a time-tested formula for successful living? Here is a simple formula that is proven and true: don't give in to peer pressure. Period.

Instead of getting lost in the crowd, you should find guidance from God. Does this sound too simple? Perhaps it is simple, but it is also the only way to reap all the marvelous riches that God has in store for you.

It's tempting to follow the crowd, but usually it's better to follow your conscience.

Criswell Freeman

Yes, Jesus Loves You!

You're blessed when you're content with just who you are—no more, no less. That's the moment you find yourselves proud owners of everything that can't be bought.

—Matthew 5:5 MSG

You've probably sung these words many times: "Jesus loves me, this I know." These happy words should remind you of this important fact: Jesus loves you very, very much.

When you invite Jesus into your heart, He will be your friend forever. If you make mistakes, He'll still be your friend. When you aren't perfect, He'll still love you. If you feel sorry or sad, He can help you feel better.

Yes, Jesus loves you . . . and you should love yourself. So the next time you feel sad about yourself . . . or something that you've done . . . remember that Jesus loves you, your family loves you, and you should feel that way, too.

Jesus loves us with fidelity, purity, constancy, and passion, no matter how imperfect we are.

Stormie Omartian

God Is Perfect; We Are Not

Since we've compiled this long and sorry record as sinners (both us and them) and proved that we are utterly incapable of living the glorious lives God wills for us, God did it for us. Out of sheer generosity he put us in right standing with himself. A pure gift. He got us out of the mess we're in and restored us to where he always wanted us to be. And he did it by means of Jesus Christ.

—Romans 3:23 MSG

If you're your own worst critic, give it up. After all, God doesn't expect you to be perfect, and if that's okay with Him, then it should be okay with you, too.

When you accepted Christ as your Savior, God accepted you for all eternity. Now, it's your turn to accept yourself. When you do, you'll feel a tremendous weight being lifted from your shoulders. And that's as it should be. After all, only one earthly being ever lived life to perfection, and He was the Son of God. The rest of us have fallen short of God's standard and need to be accepting of our own limitations as well as the limitations of others.

The happiest people in the world are not those who have no problems, but the people who have learned to live with those things that are less than perfect.

James Dobson

Think About What's Right

Keep your eyes focused on what is right. Keep looking straight ahead to what is good.

—Proverbs 4:25 ICB

In the Book of Proverbs, King Solomon gave us wonderful advice for living wisely. Solomon said that we should keep our eyes "focused on what is right." In other words, we should do our best to say and do the things that we know are pleasing to God.

The next time you're tempted to say an unkind word or to say something that isn't true, remember the advice of King Solomon. Solomon knew that it's always better to do the right thing, even when it's tempting to do otherwise. So if you know something is wrong, don't do it; instead, do what you know to be right. When you do, you'll be saving yourself a lot of trouble and you'll be obeying the Word of God.

Make God's will the focus of your life day by day. If you seek to please Him and Him alone, you'll find yourself satisfied with life.

Kay Arthur

Hope Is Contagious

I will lift up my eyes to the hills—From whence comes my help? My help comes from the Lord, Who made heaven and earth.

—Psalm 121:1-2 NKJV

The more we trust God, the better. And the more we trust God, the more secure we can feel about the future.

Hope is contagious, and hope inspired by a strong faith in God is highly contagious. So today, as you talk to friends and family members, be sure to share your hopes, your dreams, and your enthusiasm. Your positive outlook will be almost as big a blessing to them as it is to you.

Our Lord is searching for people who will make a difference. Christians dare not dissolve into the background or blend into the neutral scenery of the world.

Charles Swindoll

God is the only one who can make the valley of trouble a door of hope.

Catherine Marshall

God's Perspective

He will teach us His ways, and we shall walk in His paths.

—Isaiah 2:3 NKJV

The words of Psalm 46:10 remind us to "Be still, and know that I am God" (NKJV). When we do so, we encounter the awesome presence of our loving Heavenly Father, and we are blessed beyond words. But, when we ignore the presence of our Creator, we rob ourselves of His perspective, His peace, and His joy.

Today and every day, set aside a time to be still before God. When you do, you can face the day's complications with the wisdom and the perspective that only He can provide.

When considering the size of your problems, there are two categories that you should never worry about: the problems that are small enough for you to handle, and the ones that aren't too big for God to handle.

Marie T. Freeman

Helping to Bear the Burdens

Carry one another's burdens; in this way you will fulfill the law of Christ.

—Galatians 6:2 Holman CSB

Neighbors. We know that we are instructed to love them, and yet there's so little time…and we're so busy. No matter. As Christians, we are instructed to love our neighbors just as we love ourselves. Period.

This very day, you will encounter someone who needs a word of encouragement, or a pat on the back, or a helping hand, or a heartfelt prayer. And, if you don't reach out to that person, who will? And if you don't take the time to understand the needs of your neighbors, who will? So, today, look for a neighbor in need . . . and then do something to help. Father's orders.

He climbs highest who helps another up.

Zig Ziglar

Mercy!

Those who show mercy to others are happy, because God will show mercy to them.

—Matthew 5:7 NCV

Are you caught in the quicksand of anger? If so, you are not only disobeying God's Word, you are also wasting your time. The world holds few if any rewards for those who remain angrily focused upon the past. Still, the act of forgiveness is difficult.

If there exists even one person against whom you hold bitter feelings, it's time to forgive. Or, if you are angry with yourself for some past mistake or shortcoming, it's finally time to forgive yourself and move on. Bitterness, and regret are not part of God's plan for your life. Forgiveness is.

Give me such love for God and men as will blot out all hatred and bitterness.

Dietrich Bonhoeffer

By not forgiving, by not letting wrongs go, we aren't getting back at anyone. We are merely punishing ourselves by barricading our own hearts.

Jim Cymbala

Keep the Peace

Blessed are the peacemakers, because they will be called sons of God.

—Matthew 5:9 Holman CSB

Sometimes, it's easiest to become angry with the people we love the most. After all, we know that they'll still love us no matter how angry we become. But while it's easy to become angry at home, it's usually wrong.

The next time you're tempted to become angry with a brother, or a sister, or a parent, remember that these are the people who love you more than anybody else! Then, calm down. Because peace is always beautiful, especially when it's peace at your house.

Jesus said, "Blessed are the peacemakers: for they shall be called the children of God." Where does peacemaking begin? There can be no peace until we find peace with God.

Billy Graham

Living life with a consistent spiritual walk deeply influences those we love most.

Vonette Bright

Praise for the Father; Thanks for His Blessings

I will give You thanks with all my heart.

—Psalm 138:1 Holman CSB

Okay, you're probably a very busy person. Sometimes, you may find yourself rushing from place to place with scarcely a moment to spare. And when you're really busy, you may not take time to praise your Creator. Big mistake.

The Bible makes it clear: it pays to praise God. Worship and praise should be a part of everything you do. Otherwise, you quickly lose perspective as you fall prey to the demands of everyday life.

Do you sincerely want to know God in a more meaningful way? Then praise Him for who He is and for what He has done for you. And please don't wait until Sunday morning—praise Him all day long, every day, for as long as you live . . . and then for all eternity.

Nothing we do is more powerful or more life-changing than praising God.

Stormie Omartian

Praying to Know God

Teach me your ways, O Lord, that I may live according to your truth! Grant me purity of heart, that I may honor you.

—Psalm 86:11 NLT

Andrew Murray observed, "Some people pray just to pray, and some people pray to know God." Your job, as a maturing believer, is to pray, not out of habit or obligation, but out of a sincere desire to know your Heavenly Father. Through constant prayers, you should petition God, you should praise Him, and you should seek to discover His unfolding plans for your life.

Today, reach out to the Giver of all blessings. Turn to Him for guidance and for strength. Invite Him into every corner of your day. Ask Him to teach you and to lead you. And remember that no matter what your circumstances are, God is never far away; He is here . . . always right here. So pray.

God is a place of safety you can run to, but it helps if you are running to Him on a daily basis so that you are in familiar territory.

Stormie Omartian

Staying Out of Trouble

Don't envy bad people; don't even want to be around them. All they think about is causing a disturbance; all they talk about is making trouble.

—Proverbs 24:1-2 MSG

One way that you can feel better about yourself is by staying out of trouble. And one way that you can stay out of trouble is by making friends with people who, like you, want to do what's right.

Are your friends the kind of kids who encourage you to behave yourself? If so, you've chosen your friends wisely. But if your friends try to get you in trouble, perhaps it's time to think long and hard about making some new friends.

Whether you know it or not, you're probably going to behave like your friends behave. So pick out friends who make you want to behave better, not worse. When you do, you'll feel better about yourself . . . a whole lot better.

For better or worse, you will eventually become more and more like the people you associate with. So why not associate with people who make you better, not worse?

Marie T. Freeman

Lies Can Lead to Trouble

Your heart must not be troubled. Believe in God; believe also in Me.

—John 14:1 Holman CSB

When we tell a lie, trouble starts. Lots of trouble. But when we tell the truth—and nothing but the truth—we stop Old Man Trouble in his tracks.

When we always tell the truth, we make our worries smaller, not bigger. And that's precisely what God wants us to do.

So, if you'd like to have fewer worries and more happiness, tell the truth, the whole truth, all the time. When you do, you'll make many of your worries disappear altogether. And that's the truth!

Worry makes you forget who's in charge.

Max Lucado

We are not called to be burden-bearers, but cross-bearers and light-bearers. We must cast our burdens on the Lord.

Corrie ten Boom

The single most important element
in any human relationship
is honesty—
with oneself, with God,
and with others.

—

Catherine Marshall

Searching for the Right Kind of Treasure

Wherever your treasure is, there your heart and thoughts will also be.

—Luke 12:34 NLT

Is God a big priority for you . . . or is He an afterthought? Do you give God your best or what's left? Have you given Christ your heart, your soul, your talents, your time, and your testimony? Or are you giving Him little more than a few hours each Sunday morning?

In the book of Exodus, God warns that we should place no gods before Him (Exodus 20:3). Yet all too often, we place our Lord in second, third, or fourth place as we worship the gods of pride, money, or personal gratification. When we unwittingly place possessions or relationships above our love for the Creator, we must realign our priorities or suffer the consequences.

Does God rule your heart? Make certain that the honest answer to this question is a resounding yes. In the life of every radical believer, God comes first. And that's precisely the place that He deserves in your heart.

Jesus challenges you and me to keep our focus daily on the cross of His will if we want to be His disciples.

Anne Graham Lotz

The Size of Your Problems

Ah Lord GOD! Behold, You have made the heavens and the earth by Your great power and by Your outstretched arm! Nothing is too difficult for You.

—Jeremiah 32:17 NASB

Negative thoughts are habit-forming; thankfully, so are positive ones. With practice, you can form the habit of focusing on God's priorities and your possibilities. When you do, you'll soon discover that you will spend less time fretting about your challenges and more time praising God for His gifts.

When you call upon the Lord and prayerfully seek His will, He will give you wisdom and perspective. When you make God's priorities your priorities, He will direct your steps and calm your fears. So today and every day hereafter, pray for a sense of balance and perspective. And remember: no problems are too big for God—and that includes yours.

God has plans—not problems—for our lives.

Corrie ten Boom

It's Simple: Just Be Kind

A kind person is doing himself a favor. But a cruel person brings trouble upon himself.

—Proverbs 11:17 ICB

Never underestimate the power of kindness. You never know what kind word or gesture will significantly change someone's day, or week, or life.

Is your home like the Old West, a place "where never is heard a discouraging word and the skies are not cloudy all day" . . . or is the forecast at your house slightly cloudier than that? If your house is a place where the rule of the day is the Golden Rule, don't change a thing. Kindness starts at home, but it should never end there.

So today, slow yourself down and be alert for those who need your smile, your kind words, or your helping hand. Make kindness a centerpiece of your dealings with others. They will be blessed, and so will you.

When we do little acts of kindness that make life more bearable for someone else, we are walking in love as the Bible commands us.

Barbara Johnson

God Teaches Us

If you hide your sins, you will not succeed. If you confess and reject them, you will receive mercy.

—Proverbs 28:13 NCV

The Bible says that when people make mistakes, God corrects them. And that means that if you make a mistake, God will try to find a way to teach you how to keep from making that same mistake again.

God doesn't expect you to be perfect, but He does expect you to learn from your mistakes—NOW!

Very few things motivate us to give God our undivided attention like being faced with the negative consequences of our decisions.

Charles Stanley

Father, take our mistakes and turn them into opportunities.

Max Lucado

God is able to take mistakes, when they are committed to Him, and make of them something for our good and for His glory.

Ruth Bell Graham

Learning from the Right People

We have around us many people whose lives tell us what faith means. So let us run the race that is before us and never give up. We should remove from our lives anything that would get in the way and the sin that so easily holds us back.

—Hebrews 12:1 NCV

It has been said on many occasions that life is a team sport. So, too, is learning how to live. If we are to become mature believers—and if we seek to discover God's purposes in our everyday lives—we need worthy examples and wise mentors.

Are you walking with the wise? Are you spending time with people you admire? Are you learning how to live from people who know how to live? If you genuinely seek to walk with God, then you will walk with those who walk with Him.

The wonderful thing about God's schoolroom is that we get to grade our own papers. You see, He doesn't test us so He can learn how well we're doing. He tests us so we can discover how well we're doing.

Charles Swindoll

Your Shining Light

You are the light of the world. A city situated on a hill cannot be hidden. No one lights a lamp and puts it under a basket, but rather on a lampstand, and it gives light for all who are in the house. In the same way, let your light shine before men, so that they may see your good works and give glory to your Father in heaven.

—Matthew 5:14-16 Holman CSB

Ask yourself this question: Are you the kind of role model that you would want to copy? If so, congratulations. But if certain aspects of your behavior could stand improvement, the best day to begin your self-improvement regimen is this one. Because whether you realize it or not, people you love are watching your behavior, and they're learning how to live. You owe it to them—and to yourself—to live righteously and well.

More depends on my walk than my talk.

D. L. Moody

In serving we uncover the greatest fulfillment within and become a stellar example of a woman who knows and loves Jesus.

Vonette Bright

God's Perfect Love

This is what real love is: It is not our love for God; it is God's love for us in sending his Son to be the way to take away our sins.

—1 John 4:10 NCV

If God had a refrigerator in heaven, your picture would be on it. And that fact should make you feel very good about the person you are and the person you can become.

God's love for you is bigger and more wonderful than you can imagine, So do this, and do it right now: accept God's love with open arms and welcome His Son Jesus into your heart. When you do, you'll feel better about yourself . . . and your life will be changed forever.

God proved his love on the cross. When Christ hung, and bled, and died it was God saying to the world—I love you.

Billy Graham

We cannot protect ourselves from trouble, but we can dance through the puddles of life with a rainbow smile, twirling the only umbrella we need—the umbrella of God's love.

Barbara Johnson

Success According to God

Live the way the Lord your God has commanded you so that you may live and have what is good.

—Deuteronomy 5:33 NCV

How do you define success? Do you define it as the accumulation of stuff, stuff, and more stuff? If so, you need to reorder your priorities. Genuine success has little to do with fame or fortune; it has everything to do with God's gift of love and with His promise of salvation.

If you have allowed Christ to reign over your life, you are already a towering success in the eyes of God, but there is still more that you can do. Your task—as a believer who has been touched by the Creator's grace—is to accept the spiritual abundance and peace that He offers through the person of His Son. Then, you can share the healing message of God's love and His abundance with a world that desperately needs both. When you do, you will have reached the pinnacle of success.

Bible history is filled with people who began the race with great success but failed at the end because they disregarded God's rules.

Warren Wiersbe

New and Improved

*Your old life is dead. Your new life, which is your real life—
even though invisible to spectators—is with Christ in God.
He is your life.*

—Colossians 3:3 MSG

Has your relationship with Jesus transformed you into
an extremely different person? Hopefully so! Otherwise,
you're missing out on the joy and abundance that can be
yours through Christ.

Think, for a moment, about the "old" you, the person
you were before you invited Christ to reign over your heart.
Now, think about the "new" you, the person you've become since then. Is there a difference between the "old"
version of you and the "new-and-improved" version? There
should be! And that difference should be evident to you, to
your family, and to your friends.

When you invited Christ to reign over your heart, you
became a radically new creation. This day offers yet another
opportunity to behave yourself like that new person. When
you do, God will guide your steps and bless your endeavors
. . . forever.

Are you willing to make radical changes for Jesus? If so,
you may be certain of this fact: He's standing at the door
of your heart, patiently waiting to form an extreme, life-
altering relationship with you.

Trusting the Future to God

"I say this because I know what I am planning for you," says the Lord. "I have good plans for you, not plans to hurt you. I will give you hope and a good future."

—Jeremiah 29:11 NCV

How bright is your future? Well, if you're a faithful believer, God's plans for you are so bright that you'd better wear shades. But here's an important question: How bright do you believe your future to be? Are you expecting a terrific tomorrow, or are you dreading a terrible one? The answer you give will have a powerful impact on the way tomorrow turns out.

Do you trust in the ultimate goodness of God's plan for your life? Will you face tomorrow's challenges with optimism and hope? You should. After all, God created you for a very important reason: His reason. And you still have important work to do: His work.

Today, as you live in the present and look to the future, remember that God has an amazing plan for you. Act—and believe—accordingly.

Never be afraid to trust an unknown future to a known God.

Corrie ten Boom

Using God's Gifts

God has given gifts to each of you from his great variety of spiritual gifts. Manage them well so that God's generosity can flow through you.

—1 Peter 4:10 NLT

The gifts that you possess are gifts from the Giver of all things good. Do you have a spiritual gift? Share it. Do you have a testimony about the things that Christ has done for you? Don't leave your story untold. Do you possess financial resources? Share them. Do you have particular talents? Hone your skills and use them for God's glory.

When you obey God by sharing His gifts freely and without fanfare, you invite Him to bless you more and more. Today, be a faithful steward of your talents and treasures. And then prepare yourself for even greater blessings that are sure to come.

God is still in the process of dispensing gifts, and He uses ordinary individuals like us to develop those gifts in other people.

Howard Hendricks

Your Partnership with God

God is working in you to help you want to do and be able to do what pleases him.

—Philippians 2:13 NCV

You are God's work-in-progress. God wants to mold your heart and guide your path, but because He created you as a creature of free will, He will not force you to become His. That choice is yours alone, and it is a choice that should be reflected in every decision you make and every step you take.

Today, as you encounter the challenges of everyday life, strengthen your partnership with God through prayer, through obedience, through praise, through thanksgiving, and through service. God is the ultimate partner, and He wants to be your partner in every aspect of your life. Please don't turn Him down.

No matter what we are going through, no matter how long the waiting for answers, of one thing we may be sure. God is faithful. He keeps His promises. What He starts, He finishes…including His perfect work in us.

Gloria Gaither

Guard Your Thoughts

Be careful what you think, because your thoughts run your life.

—Proverbs 4:23 NCV

Do you try to think good thoughts about your friends, your family, and yourself? The Bible says that you should. Do you lift your hopes and your prayers to God many times each day? The Bible says that you should. Do you say "no" to people who want you to do bad things or think bad thoughts? The Bible says that you should.

The Bible teaches you to guard your thoughts against things that are hurtful or wrong. So remember this: When you turn away from bad thoughts and turn instead toward God and His Son Jesus, you will be protected . . . and you will be blessed.

People who do not develop and practice good thinking often find themselves at the mercy of their circumstances.

John Maxwell

Finishing Your Work

It is better to finish something than to start it. It is better to be patient than to be proud.

—Ecclesiastes 7:8 NCV

As you travel through life, you will undoubtedly experience your fair share of disappointments, detours, and false starts. When you do, don't become discouraged: God's not finished with you yet.

The old saying is as true today as it was when it was first spoken: "Life is a marathon, not a sprint." That's why wise travelers select a traveling companion who never tires and never falters. That partner, of course, is your Heavenly Father.

Are you tired? Ask God for strength. Are you discouraged? Believe in His promises. Are you defeated? Pray as if everything depended upon God, and work as if everything depended upon you. And finally, have faith that you play an important role in God's great plan for mankind—because you do.

If things are tough, remember that every flower that ever bloomed had to go through a whole lot of dirt to get there.

Barbara Johnson

Fear Not

They won't be afraid of bad news; their hearts are steady because they trust the Lord.

—Psalm 112:7 NCV

His adoring fans called him the "Sultan of Swat." He was Babe Ruth, the baseball player who set records for home runs and strikeouts. Babe's philosophy was simple. He said, "Never let the fear of striking out get in your way." That's smart advice on the diamond or off.

Of course it's never wise to take foolish risks (so buckle up, slow down, and don't do anything silly). But when it comes to the game of life, you should not let the fear of failure keep you from taking your swings.

Today, ask God for the courage to step beyond the boundaries of your self-doubts. Ask Him to guide you to a place where you can realize your full potential—a place where you are freed from the fear of failure. Ask Him to do His part, and promise Him that you will do your part. Don't ask Him to lead you to an "easy" place; ask Him to lead you to the "right" place . . . and remember: those two places are seldom the same.

When once we are assured that God is good, then there can be nothing left to fear.

Hannah Whitall Smith

Great Works

I assure you: The one who believes in Me will also do the works that I do. And he will do even greater works than these, because I am going to the Father.

—John 14:12 Holman CSB

Make no mistake about it: You and Jesus, working together, can do miraculous things. In fact, miraculous things are exactly what Christ intends for you to do, but He won't force you to do great things on His behalf. The decision to become a full-fledged participant in His power is a decision that you must make for yourself.

The words of John 14:12 make this promise: when you put absolute faith in Christ, you can share in His power. Today, trust the Savior's promise and expect a miracle in His name.

Where there are no good works, there is no faith. If works and love do not blossom forth, it is not genuine faith, the Gospel has not yet gained a foothold, and Christ is not yet rightly known.

Martin Luther

The Importance of Words

So then, rid yourselves of all evil, all lying, hypocrisy, jealousy, and evil speech. As newborn babies want milk, you should want the pure and simple teaching. By it you can grow up and be saved.

—1 Peter 2:1–2 NCV

How important are the words we speak? More important than we realize. Our words have echoes that extend beyond place or time. If our words are encouraging, we can lift others up; if our words are hurtful, we can hold others back.

Do you seek to be a source of encouragement to others? And, do you seek to be a worthy ambassador for Christ? If so, you must speak words that are worthy of your Savior. So avoid angry outbursts. Refrain from impulsive outpourings. Terminate tantrums. Instead, speak words of encouragement and hope to your family and friends, who, by the way, most certainly need all the hope and encouragement they can find.

Words. Do you fully understand their power? Can any of us really grasp the mighty force behind the things we say? Do we stop and think before we speak, considering the potency of the words we utter?

Joni Eareckson Tada

Fill the heart with the love of Christ
so that only truth and purity
can come out of the mouth.

—

Warren Wiersbe

Becoming a More Patient Friend

Be gentle to all, able to teach, patient.

—2 Timothy 2:24 NKJV

Friendship requires patience. From time to time, even our most considerate friends may do things that worry us, confuse us, or anger us. Why do even the most loyal friends frustrate us on occasion? Because they are human. And, it is precisely because they are human that we must, from time to time, be patient with their shortcomings (as they, too, must be patient with ours). Today and every day, let us be understanding and patient with our friends.

Friendships are living organisms at work. They continue to unfold, change, and emerge.

Barbara Johnson

Yes, the Spirit was sent to be our Counselor. Yes, Jesus speaks to us personally. But often he works through another human being.

John Eldredge

The Best Time
to Be Obedient

The one who has My commandments and keeps them is the one who loves Me. And the one who loves Me will be loved by My Father. I also will love him and will reveal Myself to him.

—John 14:21 Holman CSB

If you look in a dictionary, you'll see that the word "wisdom" means "using good judgement, and knowing what is true," But there's more: it's not enough just to know what's right; if you really want to become a wise person, you must also do what's right.

A big part of "doing what's right" is learning to be obedient . . . and the best time to start being a more obedient person is right now! Why? Because it's the wise thing to do.

Rejoicing is a matter of obedience to God—an obedience that will start you on the road to peace and contentment.

Kay Arthur

Promises You Can Trust

Do not be afraid or discouraged. For the LORD your God is with you wherever you go.

—Joshua 1:9 NLT

God has made quite a few promises to you, and He intends to keep every single one of them. You will find these promises in a book like no other: the Holy Bible. The Bible is your map for life here on earth and for life in heaven.

God's promises never fail and they never grow old. You must trust those promises and share them with your family, with your friends, and with the world . . . starting now . . . and ending never.

Gather the riches of God's promises which can strengthen you in the time when there will be no freedom.

Corrie ten Boom

Busy with Our Thoughts

Your attitude should be the same as that of Christ Jesus: Who, being in very nature God, did not consider equality with God something to be grasped, but made himself nothing, taking the very nature of a servant, being made in human likeness. And being found in appearance as a man, he humbled himself and became obedient to death—even death on a cross!

—Philippians 2:5-8 NIV

Because we are human, we are always busy with our thoughts. We simply can't help ourselves. Our brains never shut off, and even while we're sleeping, we mull things over in our minds. The question is not if we will think; the question is how will we think and what will we think about.

Today, focus your thoughts on God and His will. And if you've been plagued by pessimism and doubt, stop thinking like that! Place your faith in God and give thanks for His blessings. Think optimistically about your world and your life. It's the wise way to use your mind. And besides, since you will always be busy with your thoughts, you might as well make those thoughts pleasing (to God) and helpful (to you and yours).

Attitude is the mind's paintbrush; it can color any situation.

Barbara Johnson

Compassion and Courtesy in a Discourteous World

Now finally, all of you should be like-minded and sympathetic, should love believers, and be compassionate and humble.

—1 Peter 3:8 Holman CSB

As Christians, we are instructed to be courteous and compassionate. As believers, we are called to be gracious, humble, gentle, and kind. But sometimes, we fall short. Sometimes, amid the busyness and confusion of everyday life, we may neglect to share a kind word or a kind deed. This oversight hurts others, and it hurts us as well.

Today, slow yourself down and be alert for those who need your smile, your kind words, or your helping hand. Make kindness a centerpiece of your dealings with others. They will be blessed, and you will be, too. So make this promise to yourself and keep it: honor Christ by obeying His Golden Rule. He deserves no less. And neither, for that matter, do other people.

There are many timid souls whom we jostle morning and evening as we pass them by; but if only the kind word were spoken they might become fully persuaded.

Fanny Crosby

Whom We Should Judge

Stop judging others, and you will not be judged. Stop criticizing others, or it will all come back on you. If you forgive others, you will be forgiven.

—Luke 6:37 NLT

Here's something worth thinking about: If you judge other people harshly, God will judge you in the same way. But that's not all (thank goodness!). The Bible also promises that if you forgive other people, you, too, will be forgiven.

Are you tempted to blame people, criticize people, or judge people? If so, remember this: God is already judging what people do, and He doesn't need—or want—your help.

Christians think they are prosecuting attorneys or judges, when, in reality, God has called all of us to be witnesses.

Warren Wiersbe

Judging draws the judgment of others.

Catherine Marshall

Wisdom from the Heart

But what happens when we live God's way? He brings gifts into our lives, much the same way that fruit appears in an orchard—things like affection for others, exuberance about life, serenity. We develop a willingness to stick with things, a sense of compassion in the heart, and a conviction that a basic holiness permeates things and people. We find ourselves involved in loyal commitments, not needing to force our way in life, able to marshal and direct our energies wisely. Legalism is helpless in bringing this about; it only gets in the way.

—Galatians 5:22-23 MSG

When we genuinely open our hearts to God, He speaks to us through a small, still voice within. When He does, we can listen, or not. When we pay careful attention to the Father, he leads us along a path of His choosing, a path that leads to abundance, peace, joy, and eternal life. But when we choose to ignore God, we select a path that is not His, and we must endure the consequences of our shortsightedness.

Today, focus your thoughts and your prayers on the path that God intends for you to take. When you do, your loving Heavenly Father will speak to your heart. When He does, listen carefully . . . and trust Him.

Uniquely You

For you made us only a little lower than God, and you crowned us with glory and honor.

—Psalm 8:5 NLT

The only person in the world who's exactly like you . . . is you. And that means you're special: special to God, special to your family, special to your friends, and a special addition to God's wonderful world!

But sometimes, when you're tired, angry, dejected, or depressed, you may not feel very special. In fact, you may decide that you're the ugliest duckling in the pond, a not-very-special person . . . but whenever you think like that, you're mistaken.

The Bible says that God made you in "an amazing and wonderful way." So the next time that you start feeling like you don't measure up, remember this: when God made all the people of the earth, He only made one you. You're incredibly valuable to God, and that means that you should think of yourself as a V.I.P. (very important person). God wants you to have the best, and you deserve the best . . . you're worth it!

If you ever put a price tag on yourself, it would have to read "Jesus" because that is what God paid to save you.

Josh McDowell

Hopes, Hopes, and More Hopes

May the God of hope fill you with all joy and peace as you trust in him, so that you may overflow with hope by the power of the Holy Spirit.

—Romans 15:13 NIV

Hope is a very good thing to have . . . and to share. So make this promise to yourself and keep it: promise yourself that you'll be a hopeful person. Think good thoughts. Trust God. Become friends with Jesus. And trust your hopes, not your fears. Then, when you've filled your heart with hope and gladness, share your good thoughts with friends. They'll be better for it, and so will you.

If you can't tell whether your glass is half-empty or half-full, you don't need another glass; what you need is better eyesight . . . and a more thankful heart.

Marie T. Freeman

It never hurts your eyesight to look on the bright side of things.

Barbara Johnson

Problem-solving 101

People who do what is right may have many problems, but the Lord will solve them all.

—Psalm 34:19 NCV

Life is an exercise in problem-solving. The question is not whether we will encounter problems; the real question is how we will choose to address them. When it comes to solving the problems of everyday living, we often know precisely what needs to be done, but we may be slow in doing it—especially if what needs to be done is difficult or uncomfortable for us. So we put off till tomorrow what should be done today.

The words of Psalm 34 remind us that the Lord solves problems for "people who do what is right." And usually, doing "what is right" means doing the uncomfortable work of confronting our problems sooner rather than later. So with no further ado, let the problem-solving begin . . . now.

A faith that hasn't been tested can't be trusted.

Adrian Rogers

Why Am I Here?

May He give you what your heart desires and fulfill your whole purpose.

—Psalm 20:4 Holman CSB

"**Why did** God put me here?" It's an easy question to ask and, at times, a very difficult question to answer.

Are you earnestly trying to figure out what God wants you to do next? If so, ask Him sincerely, prayerfully, and often. When you do, God will help you find a worthy purpose for your life. Plus, you'll experience abundance, peace, joy, and power—God's power. And that's the only kind of power that really matters.

If the Lord calls you, He will equip you for the task He wants you to fulfill.

Warren Wiersbe

Only God's chosen task for you will ultimately satisfy. Do not wait until it is too late to realize the privilege of serving Him in His chosen position for you.

Beth Moore

Trust Him

Trust the Lord with all your heart, and don't depend on your own understanding. Remember the Lord in all you do, and he will give you success.

—Proverbs 3:5-6 NCV

Sometimes, things happen that we simply don't understand. But God does. And He has a reason for everything that He does.

God doesn't explain Himself in ways that we can easily comprehend. So here's what we should do: instead of trying to understanding every aspect of God's unfolding plan for our lives and our world, we must be satisfied to trust Him completely. We cannot know God's motivations, nor can we understand His actions. We can, however, trust Him, and we must.

God is God. He knows what he is doing. When you can't trace his hand, trust his heart.

Max Lucado

Faith is nothing more or less than actively trusting God.

Catherine Marshall

Faith Above Feelings

Now the just shall live by faith.

—Hebrews 10:38 NKJV

Hebrews 10:38 teaches that we should live by faith. Yet sometimes, despite our best intentions, negative feelings can rob us of the peace that would otherwise be ours through Christ. When anger or fear separates us from the spiritual blessings that God has in store, we must rethink our priorities and renew our faith. And we must place faith above feelings.

Human emotions are highly variable, decidedly unpredictable, and often unreliable. Our emotions are like the weather, only far more fickle. So we must learn to live by faith, not by the ups and downs of our own emotional roller coasters.

Sometime during this day, you will probably be gripped by a strong negative emotion. Distrust it. Reign it in. Test it. And turn it over to God. Your emotions will inevitably change; God will not. So trust Him completely as you watch your feelings slowly evaporate into thin air—which, of course, they will.

We are to live by faith, not feelings.

Kay Arthur

Beyond Envy

We can't afford to waste a minute, must not squander these precious daylight hours in frivolity and indulgence, in sleeping around and dissipation, in bickering and grabbing everything in sight. Get out of bed and get dressed! Don't loiter and linger, waiting until the very last minute. Dress yourselves in Christ, and be up and about!

—Romans 13:13-14 MSG

The Bible warns us that envy is sin. So, we must guard ourselves against the natural tendency to feel resentment and jealousy when other people experience good fortune.

As believers, we have absolutely no reason to be envious of any people on earth. After all, as Christians we are already recipients of the greatest gift in all creation: God's grace. We have been promised the gift of eternal life through God's only begotten Son, and we must count that gift as our most precious possession.

Rather than succumbing to the sin of envy, we should focus on the marvelous things that God has done for us— starting with Christ's sacrifice. And we must refrain from preoccupying ourselves with the blessings that God has chosen to give others.

So here's a surefire formula for a happier, healthier life: Count your own blessings and let your neighbors count theirs. It's the godly way to live.

Focus on the Right Things

Keep your eyes focused on what is right, and look straight ahead to what is good.

—Proverbs 4:25 NCV

Where does a good attitude begin? It starts in our hearts and works its way out from there. Jesus taught us that a pure heart is a wonderful blessing. It's up to each of us to fill our hearts with love for God, love for Jesus, and love for all people. When we do, good things happen.

Sometimes, of course, we don't feel much like feeling good. Sometimes, when we're tired, or frustrated, or angry, we simply don't want to have a good attitude. On those days when we're feeling bad, it's time to calm down . . . and rest up.

Do you want to be the best person you can be? Then you shouldn't grow tired of doing the right things . . . and you shouldn't ever grow tired of thinking the right thoughts.

Learning God's truth and getting it into our heads is one thing, but living God's truth and getting it into our characters is quite something else.

Warren Wiersbe

Enthusiasm for Life

*Do your work with enthusiasm. Work as if you were serving
the Lord, not as if you were serving only men and women.*

—Ephesians 6:7 NCV

Are you a girl who sees each day as a glorious opportunity to serve God and to do His will? Are you enthused
about life, or do you struggle through each day giving
scarcely a thought to God's blessings? Are you constantly
praising God for His gifts, and are you sharing His Good
News with the world? And are you excited about the possibilities for service that God has placed before you, whether
at home, at work, at church, or at school? You should be.

You are the recipient of Christ's sacrificial love. Accept
it enthusiastically and share it fervently. Jesus deserves
your enthusiasm; the world deserves it; and you deserve
the experience of sharing it.

We act as though comfort and luxury were the chief
requirements of life, when all we need to make us really
happy is something to be enthusiastic about.

Charles Kingsley

Body Care

Don't you know that you are God's temple and that God's Spirit lives in you?

—1 Corinthians 3:16 NCV

How do you treat your body? Do you treat it with the reverence and respect it deserves, or do you take it more or less for granted? Well, the Bible has clear instructions about the way you should take care of the miraculous body that God has given you.

God's Word teaches us that our bodies are "temples" that belong to God (1 Corinthians 6:19-20). We are commanded (not encouraged, not advised—we are commanded!) to treat our bodies with respect and honor. We do so by making wise choices and by making those choices consistently over an extended period of time.

Do you sincerely seek to improve the overall quality of your life and your health? Then promise yourself—and God—that you will begin making the kind of wise choices that will lead to a longer, healthier, happier life. The responsibility for those choices is yours. And so are the rewards.

God wants you to give Him your body. Some people do foolish things with their bodies. God wants your body as a holy sacrifice.

Warren Wiersbe

Pleasing God!

For am I now trying to win the favor of people, or God? Or am I striving to please people? If I were still trying to please people, I would not be a slave of Christ.

—Galatians 1:10 Holman CSB

Are you a people-pleaser or a God-pleaser? Hopefully, you're far more concerned with pleasing God than you are with pleasing your friends. But face facts: even if you're a devoted Christian, you're still going to feel the urge to impress your friends—and sometimes that urge will be strong.

Here's your choice: you can choose to please God first, or you can fall victim to peer pressure. The choice is yours—and so are the consequences.

When our heart's desire is to please our Lord because we love Him, there will be no time for second thoughts or second opinions.

Warren Wiersbe

You will get untold flak for prioritizing God's revealed and present will for your life over man's . . . but, boy, is it worth it.

Beth Moore

Thoughtful Words

The wise don't tell everything they know, but the foolish talk too much and are ruined.

—Proverbs 10:14 NCV

Think . . . pause . . . then speak: How wise is the person who can communicate in this way. But all too often, in the rush to have ourselves heard, we speak first and think next…with unfortunate results.

God's Word reminds us that, "Reckless words pierce like a sword, but the tongue of the wise brings healing" (Proverbs 12:18 NIV). If we seek to be a source of encouragement to our friends and family, then we must measure our words carefully. Words are important: they can hurt or heal. Words can uplift us or discourage us, and reckless words, spoken in haste, cannot be erased.

Today, seek to encourage everybody you meet. Measure your words carefully. Speak wisely, not impulsively. Remember that you have the power to heal others or to injure them, to lift others up or to hold them back. When you lift them up, your wisdom will bring healing and comfort to a world that needs both.

The things that we feel most deeply we ought to learn to be silent about, at least until we have talked them over thoroughly with God.

Elisabeth Elliot

Popularity Contests

Do you think I am trying to make people accept me? No, God is the One I am trying to please. Am I trying to please people? If I still wanted to please people, I would not be a servant of Christ.

—Galatians 1:10 NCV

If you're like most people, you seek the admiration of your neighbors and your family members. But the eagerness to please others should never overshadow your eagerness to please God. In every aspect of your life, pleasing your Heavenly Father should come first.

Would you like a time-tested formula for successful living? Here is a formula that is proven and true: Seek God's approval first and other people's approval later. Does this sound too simple? Perhaps it is simple, but it is also the only way to reap the marvelous riches that God has in store for you.

Long ago I ceased to count heads. Truth is often in the minority in this evil world.

C. H. Spurgeon

Self-defeating Anger

When you are angry, do not sin, and be sure to stop being angry before the end of the day. Do not give the devil a way to defeat you.

—Ephesians 4:26–27 NCV

When you allow yourself to become angry, you are certain to defeat at least one person: yourself. When you allow the minor frustrations of everyday life to hijack your emotions, you do harm to yourself and to your loved ones. So today and every day, guard yourself against the kind of angry thinking that inevitably takes a toll on your emotions and your relationships.

When you strike out in anger, you may miss the other person, but you will always hit yourself.

Jim Gallery

Life is too short to spend it being angry, bored, or dull.

Barbara Johnson

Bitterness and anger,
usually over trivial things,
make havoc of homes, churches,
and friendships.

—

Warren Wiersbe

Slow Down

You can't go wrong when you love others. When you add up everything in the law code, the sum total is love. But make sure that you don't get so absorbed and exhausted in taking care of all your day-by-day obligations that you lose track of the time and doze off, oblivious to God.

—Romans 13:10-11 MSG

Sure, you're a very busy girl. But here's a question: are you able to squeeze time into your hectic schedule for God? Hopefully so! But if you're one of those who rush through the day with scarcely a single moment to talk with your Creator, it's time to reshuffle your priorities.

You live in a noisy world, a world filled with distractions, frustrations, temptations, and complications. But if you allow the distractions of everyday life to distract you from God's peace, you're doing yourself a big disservice. So here's some good advice: instead of rushing nonstop through the day, slow yourself down long enough to have a few quiet minutes with God.

Nothing is more important than the time you spend with your Heavenly Father. Absolutely nothing. So be still and claim the inner peace that is your spiritual birthright: the peace of Jesus Christ. It is offered freely; it has been paid for in full; it is yours for the asking. So ask. And then share.

The Dangers of Pride

Pride leads only to shame; it is wise to be humble.

—Proverbs 11:2 NCV

The words from Proverbs 11 remind us that pride and destruction are traveling partners. But as imperfect human beings, we are tempted to puff out our chests and crow about our own accomplishments. Big mistake.

As Christians, we have a profound reason to be humble: We have been refashioned and saved by Jesus Christ, and that salvation came not because of our own good works but because of God's grace. Thus, we are not "self-made"; we are "God-made" and "Christ-saved." How, then, can we be boastful? The answer, of course, is simple: if we are honest with ourselves and with our God, we cannot be boastful. In the quiet moments, when we search the depths of our own hearts, we know that whatever "it" is, God did that. And He deserves the credit.

The Lord sends no one away empty except those who are full of themselves.

D. L. Moody

Forgive One Another

Be gentle with one another, sensitive. Forgive one another as quickly and thoroughly as God in Christ forgave you.

—Ephesians 4:32 MSG

Are you the kind of girl who has a tough time forgiving and forgetting? If so, welcome to the club. Most of us find it difficult to forgive the people who have hurt us. And that's too bad because life would be much simpler if we could forgive people "once and for all" and be done with it. Yet forgiveness is seldom that easy. Usually, the decision to forgive is straightforward, but the process of forgiving is more difficult. Forgiveness is a journey that requires effort, time, perseverance, and prayer.

If you sincerely wish to forgive someone, pray for that person. And then pray for yourself by asking God to heal your heart. Don't expect forgiveness to be easy or quick, but rest assured: with God as your partner, you can forgive . . . and you will.

Forgiveness is contagious. First you forgive them, and pretty soon, they'll forgive you, too.

Marie T. Freeman

Doing the Right Thing

Do what is right and good in the Lord's sight, so that you may prosper and so that you may enter and possess the good land the Lord your God swore to [give] your fathers.

—Deuteronomy 6:18 Holman CSB

Oswald Chambers advised, "Never support an experience which does not have God as its source, and faith in God as its result." These words serve as a powerful reminder that, as Christians, we are called to walk with God and obey His commandments. But, we live in a world that presents us with countless temptations to stray far from God's path. We Christians, when confronted with sin, have clear instructions: Walk—or better yet run—in the opposite direction.

Today, take every step of your journey with God as your traveling companion. Read His Word and follow His commandments. Support only those activities that enhance your spiritual growth. Be an example of righteous living to your friends, to your neighbors, and to your children. Then, reap the blessings that God has promised to all those who live according to His will and His Word.

Either God's Word keeps you from sin, or sin keeps you from God's Word.

Corrie ten Boom

Choices Matter

But Daniel purposed in his heart that he would not defile himself....

—Daniel 1:8 KJV

Your life is a series of choices. From the instant you wake up in the morning until the moment you nod off to sleep at night, you make lots of decisions: decisions about the things you do, decisions about the words you speak, and decisions about the thoughts you choose to think. Simply put, the quality of those decisions determines the quality of your life.

So, if you sincerely want to lead a life that is pleasing to God, you must make choices that are pleasing to Him. And you know what? He deserves no less . . . and neither, for that matter, do you.

There may be no trumpet sound or loud applause when we make a right decision, just a calm sense of resolution and peace.

Gloria Gaither

Your Attitude

Make your own attitude that of Christ Jesus.

—Philippians 2:5 Holman CSB

Your attitude can make you happy or sad, grumpy or glad, joyful or mad. And, your attitude doesn't just control the way that you think; it also controls how you behave. If you have a good attitude, you'll behave well. And if you have a bad attitude, you're more likely to mess up.

Have you spent any time thinking about the way that you think? Do you pay much attention to your attitude? Hopefully so! After all, a good attitude is better than a bad one . . . lots better.

You have more control over your attitude than you think. So do your best to make your attitude a good attitude. When you do, you'll learn that it's always better to think good thoughts, and it's always better to do good deeds. Always!

Developing a positive attitude means working continually to find what is uplifting and encouraging.

Barbara Johnson

Obeying God

But be doers of the word and not hearers only.

—James 1:22 Holman CSB

How can you show God how much you love Him? By obeying His commandments, that's how! When you follow God's rules, you show Him that you have real respect for Him and for His Son.

Sometimes, you will be tempted to disobey God, but don't do it. And sometimes you'll be tempted to disobey your parents or your teachers . . . but don't do that, either.

When your parent steps away or a teacher looks away, it's up to you to control yourself. And of this you can be sure: If you really want to control yourself, you can do it!

Happiness is obedience, and obedience is happiness.

C. H. Spurgeon

He doesn't need an abundance of words. He doesn't need a dissertation about your life. He just wants your attention. He wants your heart.

Kathy Troccoli

When You Are Hurting

But I will call on God, and the Lord will rescue me. Morning, noon, and night I plead aloud in my distress, and the Lord hears my voice.

—Psalm 55:16-17 NLT

Face it: sometimes people can be rude . . . very rude. When other people are unkind to you (or to your friends), you may be tempted to strike back, either verbally or in some other way. Don't do it! Instead, remember that God corrects other people's behaviors in His own way, and He doesn't need your help (even if you're totally convinced that He does).

As long as you live here on earth, you will face countless opportunities to lose your temper when other folks behave badly. But God has a better plan: He wants you to forgive people and move on. Remember that God has already forgiven you, so it's only right that you should be willing to forgive others.

So, when other people behave cruelly, foolishly, or impulsively—as they will from time to time—don't be hotheaded. Instead, speak up for yourself as politely as you can, and walk away. Then, forgive everybody as quickly as you can, and leave the rest up to God.

A Power Beyond Understanding

I pray also that you will have greater understanding in your heart so you will know the hope to which he has called us and that you will know how rich and glorious are the blessings God has promised his holy people. And you will know that God's power is very great for us who believe.

—Ephesians 1:18-19 NCV

Ours is a God of infinite possibilities. But sometimes, because of limited faith and limited understanding, we wrongly assume that God cannot or will not intervene in our lives. Such assumptions are simply wrong.

Are you afraid to ask God to do big things in your life? Is your faith threadbare and worn? If so, it's time to abandon your doubts and reclaim your faith in God's promises.

God's Holy Word makes it clear: absolutely nothing is impossible for the Lord. And since the Bible means what it says, you can be comforted in the knowledge that the Creator of the universe can do miraculous things in your own life and in the lives of your loved ones. Your challenge, as a believer, is to take God at His word, and to expect the miraculous.

We have a God who delights in impossibilities.

Andrew Murray

You Feel Better About Yourself When You Share

Be generous to the poor—you'll never go hungry; shut your eyes to their needs, and run a gauntlet of curses.

—Proverbs 28:27 MSG

The more you share, the quicker you'll discover this fact: Good things happen to people (like you) who are kind enough to share the blessings that God has given them.

Sharing makes you feel better about yourself. Whether you're at home or at school, remember that the best rewards go to the kids who are kind and generous—not to the people who are unkind or stingy. So do what's right: share. You'll feel lots better about yourself when you do.

Abundant living means abundant giving.

E. Stanley Jones

I have discovered that when I please Christ, I end up inadvertently serving others far more effectively.

Beth Moore

A Faith Bigger Than Fear

Do not let your hearts be troubled. Trust in God; trust also in me. In my Father's house are many rooms; if it were not so, I would have told you. I am going there to prepare a place for you.

—John 14:1-2 NIV

American clergyman Edward Everett Hale observed, "Some people bear three kinds of trouble—the ones they've had, the ones they have, and the ones they expect to have." How true. But a better strategy for you is this: accept the past, live in the present, and place the future in God's capable hands.

As you face the challenges of everyday life, you may be comforted by this fact: Trouble, of every kind, is temporary. And worries, of every kind, are temporary. But God's love is everlasting. The troubles that concern you will pass. God remains. And with these thoughts in mind, it's now time for you to place today's challenges in their proper perspective.

Today is mine. Tomorrow is none of my business. If I peer anxiously into the fog of the future, I will strain my spiritual eyes so that I will not see clearly what is required of me now.

Elisabeth Elliott

Gentle Words

Always be humble, gentle, and patient, accepting each other in love.

—Ephesians 4:2 NCV

The Bible tells us that gentle words are helpful and that cruel words are not. But sometimes, especially when we're angry or frustrated, our words and our actions may not be so gentle. Sometimes, we may say things or do things that are unkind or hurtful to others. When we do, we're wrong.

So the next time you're tempted to strike out in anger, don't. And if you want to help your family and friends, remember that gentle words are better than harsh words and good deeds are better than the other kind. Always!

I choose gentleness. Nothing is won by force. I choose to be gentle. If I raise my voice may it be only in praise. If I clench my fist, may it be only in prayer. If I make a demand, may it be only of myself.

Max Lucado

Self-esteem 101

That is why we can say with confidence, "The Lord is my helper, so I will not be afraid. What can mere mortals do to me?"

—Hebrews 13:6 NLT

Sometimes, it's hard to feel good about yourself, especially since you live in a world that keeps sending out the message that you've got to be perfect.

Are you your own worst critic? And in response to that criticism, are you constantly trying to transform yourself into a person who meets society's expectations, but not God's expectations? If so, it's time to become a little more understanding of the person in the mirror.

Millions of words have been written about various ways to improve self-esteem. Yet, maintaining a healthy self-image is, to a surprising extent, a matter of doing a few simple things: 1. Obeying. God 2. Thinking healthy thoughts. 3. Finding things to do that please your Creator and yourself. 4. Finding encouraging friends who reinforce your sense of self-worth, friends who urge you to behave yourself and believe in yourself. When you do these four things, your self-image will tend to take care of itself.

Being loved by Him whose opinion matters most gives us the security to risk loving, too—even loving ourselves.

Gloria Gaither

The Courage to Follow God

Be strong and courageous, and do the work. Don't be afraid or discouraged, for the Lord God, my God, is with you. He won't leave you or forsake you.

—1 Chronicles 28:20 Holman CSB

Because we are saved by a risen Christ, we can have hope for the future, no matter how tough our circumstances may seem. After all, God has promised that we are His throughout eternity. And, He has told us that we must place our hopes in Him.

Today, summon the courage to follow God. Even if the path seems difficult, even if your heart is fearful, trust your Heavenly Father and follow Him. Trust Him with your day and your life. Do His work, care for His children, and share His Good News. Let Him guide your steps. He will not lead you astray.

There comes a time when we simply have to face the challenges in our lives and stop backing down.

John Eldredge

Are you fearful? First, bow your head and pray for God's strength. Then, raise your head knowing that, together, you and God can handle whatever comes your way.

Jim Gallery

Starting Your Day

It is good to give thanks to the Lord, to sing praises to the Most High. It is good to proclaim your unfailing love in the morning, your faithfulness in the evening.

—Psalm 92:1-2 NLT

How do you begin your day? Do you sleep till the last possible moment without giving a single thought to God? Hopefully, that's not the case. If you're smart, you'll start your day with a prayer of thanks to your Heavenly Father.

Each new day is a gift from God, and if you're wise, you'll spend a few quiet moments thanking the Giver. It's the best way to start your day.

As we spend time reading, applying, and obeying our Bibles, the Spirit of Truth Who is also the Spirit of Jesus increasingly reveals Jesus to us.

Anne Graham Lotz

A life growing in its purity and devotion will be a more prayerful life.

E. M. Bounds

A Healthy Fear

Reverence for the Lord is the foundation of true wisdom. The rewards of wisdom come to all who obey him.

—Psalm 111:10 NLT

The Bible instructs us that a healthy fear of the Lord is the foundation of wisdom. Yet sometimes, in our short-sightedness, we fail to show respect for our Creator because we fail to obey Him. When we do, our disobedience always has consequences, and sometimes those consequences are severe.

When we honor the Father by obeying His commandments, we receive His love and His grace. Today, let us demonstrate our respect for God by developing a healthy fear of disobeying Him.

A healthy fear of God will do much to deter us from sin.

Charles Swindoll

When true believers are awed by the greatness of God and by the privilege of becoming His children, then they become sincerely motivated, effective evangelists.

Bill Hybels

The Ultimate Armor

Finally, be strong in the Lord and in his mighty power. Put on the full armor of God so that you can take your stand against the devil's schemes.

—Ephesians 6:10-11 NIV

In a world filled with dangers and temptations, God is the ultimate armor. In a world filled with misleading messages, God's Word is the ultimate truth. In a world filled with more frustrations than we can count, God's Son offers the ultimate peace. Will you accept God's peace and wear God's armor against the dangers of our world? Hopefully so.

Sometimes, in the crush of everyday life, God may seem far away, but He is not. God is everywhere you have ever been and everywhere you will ever go. He is with you night and day; He knows your thoughts and your prayers. He is your ultimate Protector. And, when you earnestly seek His protection, you will find it because He is here—always— waiting patiently for you to reach out to Him.

God will never let you sink under your circumstances. He always provide a safety net and His love always encircles.

Barbara Johnson

Using Our Gifts

I remind you to keep using the gift God gave you . . . . Now let it grow, as a small flame grows into a fire.

—2 Timothy 1:6 NCV

Face it: you've got an array of talents that need to be refined. All people possess special gifts—bestowed from the Father above—and you are no exception. But, your particular gift is no guarantee of success; it must be cultivated—by you—or it will go unused . . . and God's gift to you will be squandered.

Are you willing to do the hard work that's required to discover your talents and to develop them? If you are wise, you'll answer "yes." After all, if you don't make the most of your talents, who has the most to lose? You do!

So make a promise to yourself that you will earnestly seek to discover the talents that God has given you. Then, nourish those talents and make them grow. Finally, vow to share your gifts with the world for as long as God gives you the power to do so. After all, the best way to say "Thank You" for God's gifts is to use them.

The Lord has abundantly blessed me all of my life. I'm not trying to pay Him back for all of His wonderful gifts; I just realize that He gave them to me to give away.

Lisa Whelchel

Working Together

Work at getting along with each other and with God. Otherwise you'll never get so much as a glimpse of God.

—Hebrews 12:14 MSG

Helping other people can be fun! When you help others, you feel better about yourself—and you'll know that God approves of what you're doing.

When you learn how to cooperate with your family and friends, you'll soon discover that it's more fun when everybody works together.

So do everybody a favor: learn better ways to share and better ways to cooperate. It's the right thing to do.

The best times in life are made a thousand times better when shared with a dear friend.

Luci Swindoll

Coming together is a beginning. Keeping together is progress. Working together is success.

John Maxwell

Don't Give Up!

Thanks be to God! He gives us the victory through our Lord Jesus Christ. Therefore, my dear brothers, stand firm. Let nothing move you. Always give yourselves fully to the work of the Lord, because you know that your labor in the Lord is not in vain.

—1 Corinthians 15:57-58 NIV

Are you a girl who doesn't give up easily, or are you quick to bail out when the going gets tough? If you've developed the unfortunate habit of giving up at the first sign of trouble, it's probably time for you to have a heart-to-heart talk with that person you see every time you look in the mirror.

A well-lived life is like a marathon, not a sprint—it calls for preparation, determination, and lots of perseverance. As an example of perfect perseverance, you need look no further than your Savior, Jesus Christ.

Jesus finished what He began. Despite His suffering and despite the shame of the cross, Jesus was steadfast in His faithfulness to God. You, too, should remain faithful, especially when times are tough.

Are you facing a difficult situation? If so, remember this: whatever your problem, God can handle it. Your job is to keep persevering until He does.

Learning to Control Yourself

But endurance must do its complete work, so that you may be mature and complete, lacking nothing.

—James 1:4 Holman CSB

If you're having trouble learning how to control your actions or your emotions, you're not alone! Most people have problems with self-control from time to time, so don't be discouraged. Just remember that self-control requires practice and lots of it. So if you're a little discouraged, don't give up. Just keep working on improving your self-control until you get better at it. . . . and if you keep trying, you can be sure that sooner or later, you will get better at it.

Battles are won in the trenches, in the grit and grime of courageous determination; they are won day by day in the arena of life.

Charles Swindoll

Don't give up. Moses was once a basket case!

Anonymous

Be Respectful

Show respect for all people. Love the brothers and sisters of God's family.

—1 Peter 2:17 ICB

Are you polite and respectful to your parents and teachers? And do you do your best to treat everybody with the respect they deserve? If you want to obey God's rules, then you should be able to answer yes to these questions.

Remember this: the Bible teaches you to be a respectful person—and if it's right there in the Bible, it's certainly the right thing to do!

Although God causes all things to work together for good for His children, He still holds us accountable for our behavior.

Kay Arthur

Study the Bible and observe how the persons behaved and how God dealt with them. There is explicit teaching on every condition of life.

Corrie ten Boom

Material and Spiritual Possessions

And how do you benefit if you gain the whole world but lose your own soul in the process? Is anything worth more than your soul?

—Mark 8:36-37 NLT

Earthly riches are temporary: here today and soon gone forever. Spiritual riches, on the other hand, are permanent: ours today, ours tomorrow, ours throughout eternity. Yet all too often, we focus our thoughts and energies on the accumulation of earthly treasures, leaving precious little time to accumulate the only treasures that really matter: the spiritual kind.

Our material possessions have the potential to do great good or terrible harm, depending upon how we choose to use them. As believers, our instructions are clear: we must use our possessions in accordance with God's commandments, and we must be faithful stewards of the gifts He has seen fit to bestow upon us.

Today, let us honor God by placing no other gods before Him. God comes first; everything else comes next—and "everything else" most certainly includes all of our earthly possessions.

A Royal Law

*This royal law is found in the Scriptures: "Love your neighbor
as yourself." If you obey this law, then you are doing right.*

—James 2:8 ICB

James was the brother of Jesus and a leader of the early Christian church. In a letter that is now a part of the New Testament, James reminded his friends of a "royal law." That law is the Golden Rule.

When we treat others in the same way that we wish to be treated, we are doing the right thing. James knew it and so, of course did his brother Jesus. Now we should learn the same lesson: it's nice to be nice; it's good to be good; and it's great to be kind.

It is one of the most beautiful compensations of life that no one can sincerely try to help another without helping herself.

Barbara Johnson

When Things Go Wrong

But as for you, be strong; don't be discouraged, for your work has a reward.

—2 Chronicles 15:7 Holman CSB

Face facts: some days are more wonderful than other days. Sometimes, everything seems to go right, and on other days, many things seem to go wrong. But here's something to remember: even when you're disappointed with the way things turn out, God is near . . . and He loves you very much!

If you're disappointed, worried, sad, or afraid, you can talk to your parents and to God. And you certainly feel better when you do!

Often God has to shut a door in our face so that he can subsequently open the door through which he wants us to go.

Catherine Marshall

If we make our troubles an opportunity to learn more of God's love and His power to aid and bless, then they will teach us to have a firmer confidence in His Providence.

Billy Graham

Honesty Now

The honest person will live safely, but the one who is dishonest will be caught.

—Proverbs 10:9 ICB

Wise men and women understand that integrity is a crucial building block in the foundation of a well-lived life. Integrity is built slowly over a lifetime. It is the sum of every right decision, every honest word, every noble thought, and every heartfelt prayer. It is forged on the anvil of honorable work and polished by the twin virtues of generosity and humility. Integrity is a precious thing—difficult to build, but easy to tear down; thoughtful Christians value it and protect it at all costs.

God doesn't expect you to be perfect, but he does insist on complete honesty.

Rick Warren

Maintaining your integrity in a world of sham is no small accomplishment.

Wayne Oates

A Continual Feast?

A cheerful heart has a continual feast.

—Proverbs 15:15 Holman CSB

What is a continual feast? It's a little bit like a non-stop celebration: fun, fun, and more fun! The Bible tells us that a cheerful heart can make life like a continual feast, and that's something worth working for.

Where does cheerfulness begin? It begins inside each of us; it begins in the heart. So today and every day, let's be thankful to God for His blessings, and let's show our thanks by sharing good cheer wherever we go. This old world needs all the cheering up it can get . . . and so do we!

When we bring sunshine into the lives of others, we're warmed by it ourselves. When we spill a little happiness, it splashes on us.

Barbara Johnson

Sour godliness is the devil's religion.

John Wesley

A Thankful Heart

Enter his gates with thanksgiving; go into his courts with praise. Give thanks to him and bless his name. For the Lord is good. His unfailing love continues forever, and his faithfulness continues to each generation.

—Psalm 100:4-5 NLT

If you're like most girls on the planet, you're very busy. But, no matter how busy you are, you should never be too busy to thank God for His gifts. Your task, as a follower of the living Christ, is to praise God many times each day. Then, with gratitude in your heart, you can face your daily duties with the perspective and power that only He can provide.

When you slow down and express your gratitude to your Heavenly Father, you enrich your own life and the lives of those around you. That's why thanksgiving should become a habit, a regular part of your daily routine. Yes, God has blessed you beyond measure, and you owe Him everything, including your eternal praise.

Do you know that if at birth I had been able to make one petition, it would have been that I should be born blind? Because, when I get to heaven, the first face that shall ever gladden my sight will be that of my Savior!

Fanny Crosby

The Optimistic Christian

Make me hear joy and gladness.

—Psalm 51:8 NKJV

As a Christian, you have every reason to be optimistic about life. As John Calvin observed, "There is not one blade of grass, there is no color in this world that is not intended to make us rejoice." But, sometimes, rejoicing may be the last thing on your mind. Sometimes, you may fall prey to worry, frustration, anxiety, or sheer exhaustion. What's needed is plenty of rest, a large dose of perspective, and God's healing touch, but not necessarily in that order.

A. W. Tozer writes, "Attitude is all-important. Let the soul take a quiet attitude of faith and love toward God, and from there on, the responsibility is God's. He will make good on His commitments." These words remind us that even when the challenges of the day seem daunting, God remains steadfast. And, so must we.

Make the least of all that goes and the most of all that comes. Don't regret what is past. Cherish what you have. Look forward to all that is to come. And most important of all, rely moment by moment on Jesus Christ.

Gigi Graham Tchividjian

Finding Time for God

I am always praising you; all day long I honor you.

—Psalm 71:8 NCV

Each new day is a gift from God, and if we are wise, we spend a few quiet moments each morning thanking the Giver. Daily life is a tapestry of habits, and no habit is more important to our spiritual health than the discipline of daily prayer and devotion to the Creator. When we begin each day with our heads bowed and our hearts lifted, we remind ourselves of God's love, His protection, and His commandments. And if we are wise, we take time throughout the day to align our priorities with the teachings and commandments that God has given us through His Holy Word.

Are you thankful for God's blessings? Then give Him a gift that demonstrates your gratitude: the gift of time.

There is no way to draw closer to God unless you are in the Word of God every day. It's your compass. Your guide. You can't get where you need to go without it.

Stormie Omartian

Faith Without Works

Dear friends, do you think you'll get anywhere in this if you learn all the right words but never do anything? Does merely talking about faith indicate that a person really has it? For instance, you come upon an old friend dressed in rags and half-starved and say, "Good morning, friend! Be clothed in Christ! Be filled with the Holy Spirit!" and walk off without providing so much as a coat or a cup of soup—where does that get you? Isn't it obvious that God-talk without God-acts is outrageous nonsense?

—James 2:14-17 MSG

The central message of James' letter is the need for believers to act upon their beliefs. James' instruction is clear: "faith without works is dead." We are saved by our faith in Christ, but salvation does not signal the end of our earthly responsibilities; it marks the true beginning of our work for the Lord.

If your faith in God is strong, you will find yourself drawn toward God's work. You will serve Him, not just with words or prayers, but also with deeds. Because of your faith, you will feel compelled to do God's work—to do it gladly, faithfully, joyfully, and consistently.

Today, redouble your efforts to do God's bidding here on earth. Never have the needs—or the opportunities—been greater.

It's a Good Feeling to Obey and Forgive

For this is what love for God is: to keep His commands. Now His commands are not a burden, because whatever has been born of God conquers the world. This is the victory that has conquered the world: our faith.

—1 John 5:3-4 Holman CSB

We know that it's right to forgive other people and wrong to stay angry with them. But sometimes, it's so much easier to do the wrong thing than it is to do the right thing, especially when we're tired or frustrated.

When you do the right thing by forgiving other people, you'll feel good because you'll know that you're obeying God. And that's a very good feeling indeed. So make this promise to yourself and keep it: play by the rules—God's rules. You'll always be glad you did.

To be a Christian means to forgive the inexcusable, because God has forgiven the inexcusable in you.

C. S. Lewis

Sharing Love and Kindness

Talk and act like a person expecting to be judged by the Rule that sets us free. For if you refuse to act kindly, you can hardly expect to be treated kindly. Kind mercy wins over harsh judgment every time.

—James 2:12-13 MSG

Where does kindness start? It starts in our hearts and works its way out from there. Jesus taught us that a pure heart is a wonderful blessing. It's up to each of us to fill our hearts with love for God, love for Jesus, and love for all people. When we do, we are blessed.

Do you want to be the best person you can be? Then invite the love of Christ into your heart and share His love with your family and friends. And remember that lasting love always comes from a pure heart . . . like yours!

Keep your eyes open wide and your heart open wider.

Criswell Freeman

As you're rushing through life, take time to stop a moment, look into people's eyes, say something kind, and try to make them laugh!

Barbara Johnson

Follow Jesus

Follow Me, Jesus told them, "and I will make you into fishers of men!" Immediately they left their nets and followed Him.
—Mark 1:17-18 Holman CSB

Who will you walk with today? Do yourself a favor—walk with Jesus!

God's Word promises that when you follow in Christ's footsteps, you will learn how to behave yourself, and you'll learn how to live a good life. Jesus wants you to be a "new creation" through Him. And that's exactly what you should want for yourself, too. So talk with Jesus (through prayer) and walk with Him (by obeying His rules) today and forever.

Discipleship is a daily discipline: we follow Jesus a step at a time, a day at a time.

Warren Wiersbe

Discipleship usually brings us into the necessity of choice between duty and desire.

Elisabeth Elliot

The Bread of Life

Then Jesus said, "I am the bread that gives life. Whoever comes to me will never be hungry, and whoever believes in me will never be thirsty."

—John 6:35 NCV

He was the Son of God, but He wore a crown of thorns. He was the Savior of mankind, yet He was put to death on a roughhewn cross made of wood. He offered His healing touch to an unsaved world, and yet the same hands that had healed the sick and raised the dead were pierced with nails.

Jesus Christ, the Son of God, was born into humble circumstances. He walked this earth, not as a ruler of men, but as the Savior of mankind. His crucifixion, a torturous punishment that was intended to end His life and His reign, instead became the pivotal event in the history of all humanity.

Jesus is the bread of life. Accept His grace. Share His love. And follow His footsteps.

Jesus was the Savior Who would deliver them not only from the bondage of sin but also from meaningless wandering through life.

Anne Graham Lotz

The Power of Prayer

Therefore I say to you, whatever things you ask when you pray, believe that you receive them, and you will have them.

—Mark 11:24 NKJV

In case you've been wondering, wonder no more—God does answer your prayers. What God does not do is this: He does not always answer your prayers as soon as you might like, and He does not always answer your prayers by saying "Yes."

God isn't an order-taker, and He's not some sort of cosmic vending machine. Sometimes—even when we want something very badly—our loving Heavenly Father responds to our requests by saying "No," and we must accept His answer, even if we don't understand it.

God answers prayers not only according to our wishes but also according to His master plan. We cannot know that plan, but we can know the Planner . . . and we must trust His wisdom, His righteousness, and His love.

Of this you can be sure: God is listening, and He wants to hear from you now. So what are you waiting for?

Whatever may be our circumstances in life, may each one of us really believe that by way of the Throne we have unlimited power.

Annie Armstrong

When in Doubt . . .

Don't depend on your own wisdom. Respect the Lord and refuse to do wrong.

—Proverbs 3:7 NCV

If you're like most young people, you're busy . . . very busy. And sometimes, because so much is expected of you, you may lose perspective. Your life may seem to be spinning out of control, and the pressures of everyday living seem overwhelming. What's needed is a fresh perspective, a restored sense of balance . . . and God's wisdom.

Would you really like to become wise? If so, learning about wisdom isn't enough. You must also behave wisely. Wisdom is as wisdom does. Wisdom is determined, not by words, but by deeds.

Do you wish to walk among the wise? If so, you must walk wisely. There is simply no other way.

When you and I are related to Jesus Christ, our strength and wisdom and peace and joy and love and hope may run out, but His life rushes in to keep us filled to the brim. We are showered with blessings, not because of anything we have or have not done, but simply because of Him.

Anne Graham Lotz

Loving People Who Are Hard to Love

You have heard that it was said, You shall love your neighbor and hate your enemy. But I tell you, love your enemies, and pray for those who persecute you, so that you may be sons of your Father in heaven.

—Matthew 5:43-45 Holman CSB

Sometimes people can be rude . . . very rude. As long as you live here on earth, you will face countless opportunities to lose your temper when other folks behave badly. But God has a better plan: He wants you to forgive people and move on. Remember that God has already forgiven you, so it's only right that you should be willing to forgive others.

So here's some good advice: Forgive everybody as quickly as you can, and leave the rest up to God.

You can be sure you are abiding in Christ if you are able to have a Christlike love toward the people that irritate you the most.

Vonette Bright

What Can I Learn Today?

It takes knowledge to fill a home with rare and beautiful treasures.

—Proverbs 24:4 NCV

If we are to grow as Christians, we need both knowledge and wisdom. Knowledge is found in textbooks and in classrooms. Wisdom, on the other hand, is found in God's Holy Word and in the carefully-chosen words of loving parents, family members, and friends. Knowledge is an important building block in a well-lived life, and it pays rich dividends both personally and professionally. But, wisdom is even more important because it refashions not only the mind, but also the heart.

A big difference exists between a head full of knowledge and the words of God literally abiding in us.

Beth Moore

The more wisdom enters our hearts, the more we will be able to trust our hearts in difficult situations.

John Eldredge

Kindness Starts with You

And be kind and compassionate to one another, forgiving one another, just as God also forgave you in Christ.

—Ephesians 4:32 Holman CSB

If you're waiting for other people to be nice to you before you're nice to them, you've got it backwards. Kindness starts with you! You see, you can never control what other people will say or do, but you can control your own behavior.

The Bible tells us that we should never stop doing good deeds as long as we live. Kindness is God's way, and it should be our way, too.

The attitude of kindness is everyday stuff like a great pair of sneakers. Not frilly. Not fancy. Just plain and comfortable.

Barbara Johnson

When you launch an act of kindness out into the crosswinds of life, it will blow kindness back to you.

Dennis Swanberg

Expecting the Impossible

Is anything impossible for the Lord?

—Genesis 18:14 Holman CSB

Do you believe that God is at work in the world? And do you also believe that nothing is impossible for Him? If so, then you also believe that God is perfectly capable of doing things that you, as a mere human being with limited vision and limited understanding, would deem to be utterly impossible. And that's precisely what God does.

Since He created our universe out of nothingness, God has made a habit of doing miraculous things. And He still works miracles today. Expect Him to work miracles in your own life, and then be watchful. With God, absolutely nothing is impossible, including an amazing assortment of miracles that He stands ready, willing, and able to perform for you and yours.

If all things are possible with God, then all things are possible to him who believes in him.

Corrie ten Boom

God Makes All Things Possible

You are the God who works wonders; You revealed Your strength among the peoples.

—Psalm 77:14 Holman CSB

Sometimes, because we are imperfect human beings with limited understanding and limited faith, we place limitations on God. But, God's power has no limitations. God will work miracles in our lives if we trust Him with everything we have and everything we are. When we do, we experience the miraculous results of His endless love and His awesome power.

Do you lack the faith that God can work miracles in your own life? If so, it's time to reconsider. Are you a "Doubting Thomas," or a "Negative Nancy"? If so, you are attempting to place limitations on a God who has none. Instead, you must trust in God and trust in His power. Then, you must wait patiently . . . because something miraculous is just about to happen.

Our helplessness can be a healthy sign. This is always a good place to begin a task that seems completely impossible.

Catherine Marshall

Directing Your Thoughts!

Set your minds on what is above, not on what is on the earth.
—Colossians 3:2 Holman CSB

Do you direct your thoughts toward things that are honorable, true, and uplifting? The Bible says that you should. Do you lift your hopes and your prayers to God many times each day? The Bible says that you should. Do you turn away from bad thoughts and bad people? The Bible says that you should.

The Bible instructs you to guard your thoughts against things that are hurtful or wrong. And when you turn away from the bad and turn instead toward God and His Son Jesus, you will be protected and you will be blessed.

Surrender your mind to the Lord at the beginning of each day.

Warren Wiersbe

As we have by faith said no to sin, so we should by faith say yes to God and set our minds on things above, where Christ is seated in the heavenlies.

Vonette Bright

You Can't Please Everybody

My son, if sinners entice you, don't be persuaded.
—Proverbs 1:10 Holman CSB

Are you one of those girls who tries to please every-body in sight? If so, you'd better watch out! After all, if you worry too much about pleasing your friends, you may not worry enough about pleasing God.

Whom will you try to please today: your God or your pals? The answer to that question should be simple. Your first job is to obey God's rules . . . and that means obeying your parents, too!

So don't worry too much about pleasing your friends or neighbors. Try, instead, to please your Heavenly Father and your parents. No exceptions.

If you try to be everything to everybody, you will end up being nothing to anybody.

Vance Havner

It is impossible to please everybody. It's not impossible to please God. So try pleasing God.

Criswell Freeman

Dabblers Beware

I do not consider myself yet to have taken hold of it. But one thing I do: Forgetting what is behind and straining toward what is ahead, I press on toward the goal to win the prize for which God has called me heavenward in Christ Jesus.

—Philippians 3:13-14 NIV

Are you fired up with enthusiasm for Jesus? God has given you the gift of eternal life through His Son. In response to God's priceless gift, you are instructed to focus your thoughts, your prayers, and your energies upon God and His only begotten Son. To do so, you must resist the subtle yet powerful temptation to become a "spiritual dabbler."

A person who dabbles in the Christian faith is unwilling to place God in His rightful place: above all other things. Resist that temptation; make God the cornerstone and the touchstone of your life. When you do, He will give you all the strength and wisdom you need to live victoriously for Him.

We need to stop focusing on our lacks and stop giving out excuses and start looking at and listening to Jesus.

Anne Graham Lotz

How Often Do You Ask?

Keep asking, and it will be given to you. Keep searching, and you will find. Keep knocking, and the door will be opened to you. For everyone who asks receives, and the one who searches finds, and to the one who knocks, the door will be opened.

—Matthew 7:7-8 Holman CSB

How often do you ask for God's help? Occasionally? Once in awhile? Whenever you experience a crisis? Hopefully not. Hopefully, you have developed the habit of asking for God's assistance early and often. And hopefully, you have learned to seek His guidance in every aspect of your life.

God has promised that when you ask for His help, He will not withhold it. So ask. Ask Him to meet the needs of your day. Ask Him for wisdom. Ask Him to lead you, to protect you, and to correct you. And trust the answers He gives.

God stands at the door and waits. When you knock on His door, He answers. Your task, of course, is to seek His guidance prayerfully, confidently, and often.

God will help us become the people we are meant to be, if only we will ask Him.

Hannah Whitall Smith

In Search of Peace

Peace I leave with you. My peace I give to you. I do not give to you as the world gives. Your heart must not be troubled or fearful.

—John 14:27 Holman CSB

The beautiful words of John 14:27 give us hope: "Peace I leave with you, my peace I give unto you . . . ." Jesus offers us peace, not as the world gives, but as He alone gives. We, as believers, can accept His peace or ignore it.

When we accept the peace of Jesus Christ into our hearts, our lives are transformed. And then, because we possess the gift of peace, we can share that gift with fellow Christians, family members, and friends. If, on the other hand, we choose to ignore the gift of peace—for whatever reason—we simply cannot share what we do not possess.

Today, as a gift to yourself, to your family, and to your friends, claim the inner peace that is your spiritual birthright: the peace of Jesus Christ. It is offered freely; it has been paid for in full; it is yours for the asking. So ask. And then share.

When we do what is right, we have contentment, peace, and happiness.

Beverly LaHaye

Mountain-moving Faith

For I assure you: If you have faith the size of a mustard seed, you will tell this mountain, "Move from here to there," and it will move. Nothing will be impossible for you.

—Matthew 17:20 Holman CSB

Have you ever felt your faith in God slipping away? If so, you are not alone. Every life—including yours—is a series of successes and failures, celebrations and disappointments, joys and sorrows. But even when we feel very distant from God, God is never distant from us.

Jesus taught His disciples that if they had faith, they could move mountains. You can too. When you place your faith, your trust, indeed your life in the hands of Christ Jesus, you'll be amazed at the marvelous things He can do with you and through you. So strengthen your faith through praise, through worship, through Bible study, and through prayer. And trust God's plans. With Him, all things are possible, and He stands ready to open a world of possibilities to you if you have faith.

Faith is to believe what you do not see; the reward of this faith is to see what you believe.

St. Augustine

How Do They Know?

Even a child is known by his behavior. His actions show if he is innocent and good.

—Proverbs 20:11 ICB

How do people know that you're a Christian? Well, you can tell them, of course. And make no mistake about it: talking about your faith in God is a very good thing to do. But simply telling people about Jesus isn't enough. You must also be willing to show people how a real Christian (like you) should behave. Does that sound like a big responsibility? It is . . . but you can do it!

In our faith we follow in someone's steps. In our faith we leave footprints to guide others. It's the principle of discipleship.

Max Lucado

We urgently need people who encourage and inspire us to move toward God and away from the world's enticing pleasures.

Jim Cymbala

When Times Are Tough

I have told you these things so that in Me you may have peace. In the world you have suffering. But take courage! I have conquered the world.

—John 16:33 Holman CSB

The Bible promises this: tough times are temporary but God's love is not—God's love lasts forever. So what does that mean to you? Just this: From time to time, everybody faces tough times, and so will you. And when tough times arrive, God will always stand ready to protect you and heal you.

Psalm 147 promises, "He heals the brokenhearted" (v. 3, NIV), but Psalm 147 doesn't say that He heals them instantly. Usually, it takes time (and maybe even a little help from you) for God to fix things. So if you're facing tough times, face them with God by your side. If you find yourself in any kind of trouble, pray about it and ask God for help. And be patient. God will work things out, just as He has promised, but He will do it in His own way and in His own time.

Often the trials we mourn are really gateways into the good things we long for.

Hannah Whitall Smith

Praising God's Glorious Creation

The heavens declare the glory of God, and the sky proclaims the work of His hands.

—Psalm 19:1 Holman CSB

Each morning, the sun rises upon a glorious world that is a physical demonstration of God's infinite power and His infinite love. And yet we're sometimes too busy to notice.

We live in a society filled with more distractions than we can possibly count and more obligations than we can possibly meet. Is it any wonder, then, that we often overlook God's handiwork as we rush from place to place, giving scarcely a single thought to the beauty that surrounds us?

Today, take time to really observe the world around you. Take time to offer a prayer of thanks for the sky above and the beauty that lies beneath it. And take time to ponder the miracle of God's creation. The time you spend celebrating God's wonderful world is always time well spent.

The more carefully you inspect God's unfolding universe, the more beautiful it becomes.

Marie T. Freeman

God's Timetable

There is an occasion for everything, and a time for every activity under heaven.

—Ecclesiastes 3:1 Holman CSB

As busy people living in a fast-paced world, many of us find that waiting quietly for God is difficult. Why? Because we are imperfect human beings seeking to live according to our own timetables, not God's. In our better moments, we realize that patience is not only a virtue, but it is also a commandment from the Creator.

God instructs us to be patient in all things. We must be patient with our families, with our friends, and with our acquaintances. We must also be patient with our Heavenly Father as He unfolds His plan for our lives. And that's as it should be. After all, think how patient God has been with us.

By his wisdom, he orders his delays so that they prove to be far better than our hurries.

C. H. Spurgeon

Waiting is the hardest kind of work, but God knows best, and we may joyfully leave all in His hands.

Lottie Moon

It's Good for You

So I recommend having fun, because there is nothing better for people to do in this world than to eat, drink, and enjoy life. That way they will experience some happiness along with all the hard work God gives them.

—Ecclesiastes 8:15 NLT

Sometimes, we may feel guilty about having fun when some people around the world are not having any fun at all. But God doesn't want us to spend our lives moping around with frowns on our faces. Far from it! God tells us that a happy heart is a very good thing to have.

So if you're afraid to laugh out loud, don't be. Remember that God wouldn't have given you the gift of laughter if He hadn't intended for you to use it. And remember: if you're laughing, that does not mean that you're unconcerned about people who may be hurting. It simply means that you've taken a little time to have fun, and that's good because God wants you to have a cheerful heart.

Whence comes this idea that if what we are doing is fun, it can't be God's will? The God who made giraffes, a baby's fingernails, a puppy's tail, a crooknecked squash, the bobwhite's call, and a young girl's giggle, has a sense of humor. Make no mistake about that.

Catherine Marshall

This Is the Day

This is the day the Lord has made; let us rejoice and be glad in it.

—Psalm 118:24 Holman CSB

Are you basically a thankful person? Do you appreciate the stuff you've got and the life that you're privileged to live? You most certainly should be thankful. After all, when you stop to think about it, God has given you more blessings than you can count. So the question of the day is this: will you slow down long enough to thank your Heavenly Father . . . or not?

Sometimes, life here on earth can be complicated, demanding, and frustrating. When the demands of life leave you rushing from place to place with scarcely a moment to spare, you may fail to pause and thank your Creator for the countless blessings He has given you. Failing to thank God is understandable . . . but it's wrong.

God's Word makes it clear: a wise heart is a thankful heart. Period. Your Heavenly Father has blessed you beyond measure, and you owe Him everything, including your thanks. God is always listening—are you willing to say thanks? It's up to you, and the next move is yours.

The Power of Our Thoughts

People's thoughts can be like a deep well, but someone with understanding can find the wisdom there.

—Proverbs 20:5 NCV

Our thoughts have the power to shape our lives—for better or for worse. Thoughts have the power to lift our spirits, to improve our circumstances, and to strengthen our relationship with the Creator. But, our thoughts also have the power to cause us great harm if we focus too intently upon those things that distance us from God.

Today, make your thoughts an offering to God. Seek—by the things you think and the actions you take—to honor Him and serve Him. He deserves no less. And neither, for that matter, do you.

The things we think are the things that feed our souls. If we think on pure and lovely things, we shall grow pure and lovely like them; and the converse is equally true.

Hannah Whitall Smith

It is the thoughts and intents of the heart that shape a person's life.

John Eldredge

I became aware of one very
important concept I had
missed before:
my attitude
—not my circumstances—
was what was making me unhappy.
—

Vonette Bright

The Joys of a Clear Conscience

Let us come near to God with a sincere heart and a sure faith, because we have been made free from a guilty conscience, and our bodies have been washed with pure water.

—Hebrews 10:22 NCV

Few things in life torment us more than a guilty conscience. And, few things in life provide more contentment than the knowledge that we are obeying God's commandments. A clear conscience is one of the rewards we earn when we obey God's Word and follow His will. When we follow God's will and accept His gift of salvation, our earthly rewards are never-ceasing, and our heavenly rewards are everlasting.

God desires that we become spiritually healthy enough through faith to have a conscience that rightly interprets the work of the Holy Spirit.

Beth Moore

When You Don't Know What to Say

Watch the way you talk. Let nothing foul or dirty come out of your mouth. Say only what helps, each word a gift.
—Ephesians 4:29 MSG

Sometimes, it's hard to know exactly what to say. And sometimes, it can be very tempting to say something that isn't true—or something that isn't polite. But when you say things you shouldn't say, you'll regret it later.

So make this promise to yourself, and keep it—promise to think about the things you say before you say them. And whatever you do, always tell the truth. When you do these things, you'll be doing yourself a big favor, and you'll be obeying the Word of God.

When you talk, choose the very same words that you would use if Jesus were looking over your shoulder. Because He is.

Marie T. Freeman

Change the heart, and you change the speech.

Warren Wiersbe

Really Living Means Really Loving

And may the Lord cause you to increase and overflow with love for one another and for everyone, just as we also do for you.

—1 Thessalonians 3:12 Holman CSB

Christ's words are clear: we are to love God first, and secondly, we are to love others as we love ourselves (Matthew 22:37-40). These two commands are seldom easy, and because we are far from perfect, we often fall short. But God's Holy Word commands us to try.

The Christian path is an exercise in love and forgiveness. If we are to walk in Christ's footsteps, we must forgive those who have done us harm, and we must accept Christ's love by sharing it freely with family, friends, neighbors, and strangers.

It is when we come to the Lord in our nothingness, our powerlessness and our helplessness that He then enables us to love in a way which, without Him, would be absolutely impossible.

Elisabeth Elliot

Prayerful Patience

The Lord is good to those whose hope is in him, to the one who seeks him; it is good to wait quietly for the salvation of the Lord.

—Lamentations 3:25-26 NIV

Lamentations 3:25-26 reminds us that it is good to wait quietly for God. But for most of us, waiting patiently for Him is difficult. Why? Because we are fallible human beings with a long list of earthly desires and a definite timetable for obtaining them.

The next time you find yourself impatiently waiting for God to reveal Himself, remember that the world unfolds according to His timetable, not ours. Sometimes, we must wait, and when we do, we should do so quietly and patiently. And, as we consider God's love for us and the perfection of His plans, we can be comforted in the certain knowledge that His timing is perfect, even if our patience is not.

Forgiveness is a stunning principle, your ticket out of hate and fear and chaos.

Barbara Johnson

What Your Conscience Says About Forgiveness

Now the goal of our instruction is love from a pure heart, a good conscience, and a sincere faith.

—1 Timothy 1:5 Holman CSB

Your conscience will usually tell you what to do and when to do it. Trust that feeling. Your conscience is usually right.

If you listen to your conscience, it won't be as hard for you to forgive people. Why? Because forgiving other people is the right thing to do. And, it's what God wants you to do. And it's what your conscience tells you to do. So what are you waiting for?

The fire of anger, if not quenched by loving forgiveness, will spread and defile and destroy the work of God.

Warren Wiersbe

Most of us follow our conscience as we follow a wheelbarrow. We push it in front of us in the direction we want to go.

Billy Graham

Asking and Accepting

So I say to you, keep asking, and it will be given to you. Keep searching, and you will find. Keep knocking, and the door will be opened to you.

—Luke 11:9 Holman CSB

God gives the gifts; we, as believers, should accept them—but oftentimes, we don't. Why? Because we fail to trust our Heavenly Father completely, and because we are, at times, surprisingly stubborn. Luke 11 teaches us that God does not withhold spiritual gifts from those who ask. Our obligation, quite simply, is to ask for them.

Are you asking God to move mountains in your life, or are you expecting Him to stumble over molehills? Whatever the size of your challenges, God is big enough to handle them. Ask for His help today, with faith and with fervor, and then watch in amazement as your mountains begin to move.

By asking in Jesus' name, we're making a request not only in His authority, but also for His interests and His benefit.

Shirley Dobson

When Friends Behave Badly

Whoever walks with the wise will become wise; whoever walks with fools will suffer harm.

—Proverbs 13:20 NLT

If you're like most people, you have probably been tempted to "go along with the crowd" . . . even when the crowd was misbehaving. But here's something to think about: just because your friends may be misbehaving doesn't mean that you have to misbehave, too.

When people behave badly, they can spoil things in a hurry. So make sure that they don't spoil things for you.

So, if your friends misbehave, don't copy them! Instead, do the right thing. You'll be glad you did . . . and so will God!

Pride opens the door to every other sin, for once we are more concerned with our reputation than our character, there is no end to the things we will do just to make ourselves "look good" before others.

Warren Wiersbe

Building Character, Moment by Moment

May integrity and uprightness protect me, because my hope is in you.

—Psalm 25:21 NIV

It has been said that character is what we are when nobody is watching. How true. But, as Bill Hybels correctly observed, "Every secret act of character, conviction, and courage has been observed in living color by our omniscient God." And isn't that a sobering thought?

When we do things that we know aren't right, we try to hide our misdeeds from family members and friends. But even then, God is watching.

If you sincerely wish to walk with God, you must seek, to the best of your ability, to follow His commandments. When you do, your character will take care of itself…and you won't need to look over your shoulder to see who, besides God, is watching.

Every time you refuse to face up to life and its problems, you weaken your character.

E. Stanley Jones

The Time to Do the Right Thing Is Now

So don't get tired of doing what is good. Don't get discouraged and give up, for we will reap a harvest of blessing at the appropriate time.

—Galatians 6:9 NLT

The old saying is both familiar and true: actions speak louder than words. And as believers, we must beware: our actions should always give credence to the changes that Christ can make in the lives of those who walk with Him.

God calls upon each of us to act in accordance with His will and with respect for His commandments. If we are to be responsible believers, we must realize that it is never enough simply to hear the instructions of God; we must also live by them. And it is never enough to wait idly by while others do God's work here on earth; we, too, must act. Doing God's work is a responsibility that each of us must bear, and when we do, our loving Heavenly Father rewards our efforts with a bountiful harvest.

We spend our lives dreaming of the future, not realizing that a little of it slips away every day.

Barbara Johnson

Pray as if it's all up to God,
and work as if it's all up to you.

—

Anonymous

Finding the Purpose Beneath the Problem

Be joyful because you have hope. Be patient when trouble comes, and pray at all times.

—Romans 12:12 NCV

Hidden beneath every problem is the seed of a solution—God's solution. Your challenge, as a faithful believer, is to trust God's providence and seek His solutions. When you do, you will eventually discover that God does nothing without a very good reason: His reason.

Are you willing to faithfully trust God on good days and bad ones? Hopefully so, because an important part of walking with God is finding His purpose in the midst of your problems.

Looking back, I can see that the most exciting events of my life have all risen out of trouble.

Catherine Marshall

Often the trials we mourn are really gateways into the good things we long for.

Hannah Whitall Smith

Obedience to God

But prove yourselves doers of the word, and not merely hearers.

—James 1:22 NASB

God's commandments are not "suggestions," and they are not "helpful hints." They are, instead, immutable laws which, if followed, lead to repentance, salvation, and abundance. But if you choose to disobey the commandments of your Heavenly Father or the teachings of His Son, you will most surely reap a harvest of regret.

The formula for a successful life is surprisingly straightforward: Study God's Word and obey it. Does this sound too simple? Perhaps it is simple, but it is also the only way to reap the marvelous riches that God has in store for You.

Obedience is the outward expression of your love of God.

Henry Blackaby

I don't always like His decisions, but when I choose to obey Him, the act of obedience still "counts" with Him even if I'm not thrilled about it.

Beth Moore

Our Problems = God's Opportunities

As for God, his way is perfect. All the LORD's promises prove true. He is a shield for all who look to him for protection.

—Psalm 18:30 NLT

Here's a riddle: What is it that is too unimportant to pray about yet too big for God to handle? The answer, of course, is: "nothing." Yet sometimes, when the challenges of the day seem overwhelming, we may spend more time worrying about our troubles than praying about them. And, we may spend more time fretting about our problems than solving them. A far better strategy is to pray as if everything depended entirely upon God and to work as if everything depended entirely upon us.

What we see as problems God sees as opportunities. And if we are to trust Him completely, we must acknowledge that even when our own vision is dreadfully impaired, His vision is perfect. Today and every day, let us trust God by courageously confronting the things that we see as problems and He sees as possibilities.

Each problem is a God-appointed instructor.

Charles Swindoll

Nobody's Perfect

For everything created by God is good, and nothing should be rejected if it is received with thanksgiving.

—1 Timothy 4:4 Holman CSB

Face facts: nobody's perfect . . . not even you! And remember this: it's perfectly okay not to be perfect. In fact, God doesn't expect you to be perfect, and you shouldn't expect yourself to be perfect, either.

Are you one of those people who can't stand to make a mistake? Do you think that you must please everybody all the time? When you make a mess of things, do you become terribly upset? If so, here's some advice: DON'T BE SO HARD ON YOURSELF! Mistakes happen . . . and besides, if you learn something from your mistakes, you'll become a better person.

The greatest destroyer of good works is the desire to do great works.

C. H. Spurgeon

Quiet Time

Rest in God alone, my soul, for my hope comes from Him.

—Psalm 62:5 Holman CSB

The world can be a noisy place, a place filled to the brim with distractions, interruptions, and frustrations. And if you're not careful, the struggles and stresses of everyday living can rob you of the peace that should rightfully be yours because of your personal relationship with Christ. So take time each day to spend quiet time with your Savior. When you do, those moments of silence will enable you to participate more fully in the only source of peace that endures: God's peace.

In the soul-searching of our lives, we are to stay quiet so we can hear Him say all that He wants to say to us in our hearts.

Charles Swindoll

Silence is as fit a garment for devotion as any other language.

C. H. Spurgeon

Include God in Your Plans

Depend on the Lord in whatever you do, and your plans will succeed.

—Proverbs 16:3 NCV

Would you like a formula for successful living that never fails? Here it is: Include God in every aspect of your life's journey, including the plans that you make and the steps that you take. But beware: as you make plans for the days and weeks ahead, you may become sidetracked by the demands of everyday living.

If you allow the world to establish your priorities, you will eventually become discouraged, or disappointed, or both. But if you genuinely seek God's will for every important decision that you make, your loving Heavenly Father will guide your steps and enrich your life. So as you plan your day, remember that every good plan should start with God, including yours.

A #2 pencil and a dream can take you anywhere.

Joyce Meyer

Keeping Possessions in Perspective

No one can serve two masters. The person will hate one master and love the other, or will follow one master and refuse to follow the other. You cannot serve both God and worldly riches.

—Matthew 6:24 NCV

"So much stuff to shop for, and so little time . . . ." These words seem to describe the priorities of our 21st-century world. Hopefully, you're not building your life around your next visit to the local mall—but you can be sure that many people are!

Our society is in love with money and the things that money can buy. God is not. God cares about people, not possessions, and so must we. We must, to the best of our abilities, love our neighbors as ourselves, and we must, to the best of our abilities, resist the mighty temptation to place possessions ahead of people.

Money, in and of itself, is not evil; worshipping money is. So today, as you prioritize matters of importance for you and yours, remember that God is almighty, but the dollar is not.

Why is love of gold more potent than love of souls?

Lottie Moon

With All Your Heart and Soul

Love the LORD your God with all your heart and with all your soul and with all your strength.

—Deuteronomy 6:5 NIV

God's love for you is bigger and stronger than you can imagine. God's love for you is so great that He sent His only Son to this earth to die for your sins and to offer you the priceless gift of eternal life. Now, you must decide whether or not to accept God's gift. Will you ignore it or embrace it? Will you return it or neglect it? Will you accept Christ's love and build a lifelong relationship with Him, or will you turn away from Him and take a different path?

Your decision to allow Christ to reign over your heart is the pivotal decision of your life. It is a decision that you cannot ignore. It is a decision that is yours and yours alone. Accept God's gift now: allow His Son to preside over your heart, your thoughts, and your life, starting this very instant.

It's your heart that Jesus longs for: your will to be made His own with self on the cross forever, and Jesus alone on the throne.

Ruth Bell Graham

Too Many Temptations

But remember that the temptations that come into your life are no different from what others experience. And God is faithful. He will keep the temptation from becoming so strong that you can't stand up against it. When you are tempted, he will show you a way out so that you will not give in to it.

—1 Corinthians 10:13 NLT

How hard is it to bump into temptation in this crazy world? Not very hard. The devil is working overtime, and he's in your neighborhood right now, looking for victims.

In a letter to believers, Peter offers a stern warning: "Your adversary, the devil, prowls around like a roaring lion, seeking someone to devour" (1 Peter 5:8 NASB). What was true in New Testament times is equally true in our own. Satan tempts his prey and then devours them (and it's up to you—and only you—to make sure that you're not one of the ones being devoured!).

As a girl who seeks a life-changing relationship with Jesus, you must beware because temptations are everywhere. Satan is determined to win; you must be equally determined that he does not.

We, as God's people, are not only to stay far away from sin and sinners who would entice us, but we are to be so like our God that we mourn over sin.

Kay Arthur

Finding (and Trusting) Mentors

A wise man will listen and increase his learning, and a discerning man will obtain guidance.

—Proverbs 1:5 Holman CSB

Do you want to become wise? Then you must acknowledge that you are not wise enough on your own. When you face an important decision, you must first study God's Word, and you should also seek the counsel of trusted friends and mentors.

When we arrive at the inevitable crossroads of life, God inevitably sends righteous men and women to guide us if we let them. If we are willing to listen and to learn, then we, too, will become wise. And God will bless our endeavors.

God makes wise people available to you. Your job is to listen and learn.

Criswell Freeman

Do you want to be wise? Choose wise friends.

Charles Swindoll

Self-Control and Patience

All athletes practice strict self-control. They do it to win a prize that will fade away, but we do it for an eternal prize.

—1 Corinthians 9:25 NLT

The Bible tells us that self-control and patience are very good things to have. But for most of us, self-control and patience can also be very hard things to learn.

Are you having trouble being patient? And are you having trouble slowing down long enough to think before you act? If so, remember that self-control takes practice, and lots of it, so keep trying. And if you make a mistake, don't be too upset. After all, if you're going to be a really patient person, you shouldn't just be patient with others; you should also be patient with yourself.

Your thoughts are the determining factor as to whose mold you are conformed to. Control your thoughts and you control the direction of your life.

Charles Stanley

How They Know
That We Know

*Here's how we can be sure that we know God in the right way:
Keep his commandments. If someone claims, "I know him
well!" but doesn't keep his commandments, he's obviously a
liar. His life doesn't match his words. But the one who keeps
God's word is the person in whom we see God's mature love.
This is the only way to be sure we're in God. Anyone who
claims to be intimate with God ought to live the same kind of
life Jesus lived.*

—1 John 2:3-6 MSG

How do others know that we are followers of Christ?
By our words and by our actions. And when it comes to
proclaiming our faith, the actions we take are far more important than the proclamations we make.

Is your conduct a worthy example for believers and
non-believers alike? Is your behavior a testimony to the
spiritual abundance that is available to those who allow
Christ to reign over their hearts? If so, you are wise: congratulations. But if you're like most of us, then you know
that some important aspect of your life could stand improvement. If so, today is the perfect day to make yourself
a living, breathing example of the wonderful changes that
Christ can make in the lives of those who choose to walk
with Him.

The Company You Keep

Do not be deceived: "Bad company corrupts good morals."
—1 Corinthians 15:33 Holman CSB

Our world is filled with pressures: some good, some bad. The pressures that we feel to follow God's will and to behave responsibly are positive pressures. God places them on our hearts, and He intends that we act accordingly. But we also face different pressures, ones that are definitely not from God. When we feel pressured to do things—or even to think thoughts—that lead us away from God, we must beware.

Society seeks to mold us into the cookie-cutter images that are the product of the modern media. God seeks to mold us into new beings, new creations through Christ, beings that are most certainly not conformed to this world. If we are to please God, we must resist the pressures that society seeks to impose upon us, and we must conform ourselves, instead, to His will, to His path, and to His Son.

It is comfortable to know that we are responsible to God and not to man. It is a small matter to be judged of man's judgement.

Lottie Moon

Mary, Martha, and the Master

You will teach me how to live a holy life. Being with you will fill me with joy; at your right hand I will find pleasure forever.
—Psalm 16:11 NCV

Martha and Mary were sisters who both loved Jesus, but they showed their love in different ways. Mary sat at the Master's feet, taking in every word. Martha, meanwhile, busied herself with preparations for the meal to come. When Martha asked Jesus if He was concerned about Mary's failure to help, Jesus replied, "Mary has chosen the better thing, and it will never be taken away from her" (Luke 10:42 NCV). The implication is clear: as believers, we must spend time with Jesus before we spend time for him. But, once we have placed Christ where He belongs—at the center of our hearts—we must go about the business of serving the One who has saved us.

How can we serve Christ? By sharing His message, His mercy, and His love with those who cross our paths. Everywhere we look, it seems, the needs are great and so are the temptations. Still, our challenge is clear: we must love God, obey His commandments, trust His Son, and serve His children. When we do, we claim spiritual treasures that will endure forever.

Holiness Before Happiness

Blessed are those who hunger and thirst for righteousness, because they will be filled.

—Matthew 5:6 Holman CSB

Because you are an imperfect human being, you are not "perfectly" happy—and that's perfectly okay with God. He is far less concerned with your happiness than He is with your holiness.

God continuously reveals Himself in everyday life, but He does not do so in order to make you contented; He does so in order to lead you to His Son. So don't be overly concerned with your current level of happiness: it will change. Be more concerned with the current state of your relationship with Christ: He does not change. And because your Savior transcends time and space, you can be comforted in the knowledge that in the end, His joy will become your joy . . . for all eternity.

Holiness is not an impossibility for any of us.

Elisabeth Elliot

Be Generous Now

God loves the person who gives happily.

—2 Corinthians 9:7 ICB

How fortunate we are to live in a land of opportunities and possibilities. But, for many people around the world, opportunities are scarce at best. In too many corners of the globe, hardworking men and women struggle mightily to provide food and shelter for their families.

The man from Galilee advised His followers, "I tell you the truth, whatever you did for one of the least of these brothers of mine, you did for me" (Matthew 25:40 NIV). Jesus' words still apply.

When we care for the downtrodden, we follow in the footsteps of Christ. And, when we show compassion for those who suffer, we abide by the commandments of the One who created us. May we Americans hear the Word of God . . . and may we follow it.

When somebody needs a helping hand, he doesn't need it tomorrow or the next day. He needs it now, and that's exactly when you should offer to help. Good deeds, if they are really good, happen sooner rather than later.

Marie T. Freeman

Following in the Footsteps

Whoever serves me must follow me. Then my servant will be with me everywhere I am. My Father will honor anyone who serves me.

—John 12:26 NCV

If you genuinely want to make choices that are pleasing to God, you must ask yourself this question: "How does God want me to serve others?"

Whatever your age, wherever you happen to be, you may be certain of this: service to others is an integral part of God's plan for your life.

Every single day of your life, including this one, God will give you opportunities to serve Him by serving other people. Welcome those opportunities with open arms. They are God's gift to you, His way of allowing you to achieve greatness in His kingdom.

The heaviest end of the cross lies ever on His shoulders. If He bids us carry a burden, He carries it also.

C. H. Spurgeon

Have thy tools ready; God will find thee work.

Charles Kingsley

Living Above
the Daily Whine

Do everything readily and cheerfully—no bickering, no second-guessing allowed! Go out into the world uncorrupted, a breath of fresh air in this squalid and polluted society. Provide people with a glimpse of good living and of the living God. Carry the light-giving Message into the night.

—Philippians 2:14-15 MSG

Sometimes, we lose sight of our blessings. Ironically, most of us have more blessings than we can count, but we may still find reasons to complain about the minor frustrations of everyday life. To do so, of course, is not only wrong; it is also the pinnacle of shortsightedness and a serious roadblock on the path to spiritual abundance.

Are you tempted to complain about the inevitable minor frustrations of everyday living? Don't do it! Today and every day, make it a practice to count your blessings, not your hardships. It's the truly decent way to live.

Some people complain that God put thorns on roses, while others praise Him for putting roses on thorns.

Anonymous

Trusting God's Word

But He answered, "It is written: Man must not live on bread alone, but on every word that comes from the mouth of God."
—Matthew 4:4 Holman CSB

The Bible is unlike any other book. A. W. Tozer wrote, "The purpose of the Bible is to bring people to Christ, to make them holy and prepare them for heaven. In this it is unique among books, and it always fulfills its purpose."

As Christians, we are called upon to share God's Holy Word with a world in desperate need of His healing hand. The Bible is a priceless gift, a tool for Christians to use as they share the Good News of their Savior, Christ Jesus. Too many Christians, however, keep their spiritual tool kits tightly closed and out of sight.

Jonathan Edwards advised, "Be assiduous in reading the Holy Scriptures. This is the fountain whence all knowledge in divinity must be derived. Therefore let not this treasure lie by you neglected." God's Holy Word is, indeed, a priceless, one-of-a-kind treasure. Handle it with care, but more importantly, handle it every day.

Weave the unveiling fabric of God's word through your heart and mind. It will hold strong, even if the rest of life unravels.

Gigi Graham Tchividjian

What Kind of Example?

You should be an example to the believers in speech, in conduct, in love, in faith, in purity.

—1 Timothy 4:12 Holman CSB

Whether we like it or not, all of us are examples. The question is not whether we will be examples to our families and friends; the question is simply, what kind of examples will we be?

What kind of example are you? Are you the kind of girl whose life serves as a powerful example of righteousness? Are you a young woman whose behavior serves as a positive role model for younger folks? Are you the kind of girl whose actions, day in and day out, are honorable, ethical, and admirable? If so, you are not only blessed by God, but you are also a powerful force for good in a world that desperately needs positive influences such as yours.

You can never separate a leader's actions from his character.

John Maxwell

In your desire to share the gospel, you may be the only Jesus someone else will ever meet. Be real and be involved with people.

Barbara Johnson

The Right Kind of Peer Pressure

Therefore, my dear brothers, be steadfast, immovable, always abounding in the Lord's work, knowing that your labor in the Lord is not in vain.

—1 Corinthians 15:58 Holman CSB

Some friends encourage us to obey God—these friends help us make wise choices. Other friends put us in situations where we are tempted to disobey God—these friends tempt us to make unwise choices.

Are you hanging out with people who make you a better Christian, or are you spending time with people who encourage you to stray from your faith? The answer to this question will help determine the condition of your spiritual health. One of the best ways to ensure that you follow Christ is to find fellow believers who are willing to follow Him with you.

A friend is one who makes me do my best.

Oswald Chambers

Every Day Is a Special Day

David and the whole house of Israel were celebrating before the Lord.

—2 Samuel 6:5 Holman CSB

Today is a day of celebration, and hopefully, you do feel like celebrating! After all, today (like every other day) should be a special time to thank God for all the wonderful things He has given you.

So don't wait for birthdays or holidays—make every day a special day, including this one. Take time to pause and thank God for His gifts. He deserves your thanks, and you deserve to celebrate!

If you can forgive the person you were, accept the person you are, and believe in the person you will become, you are headed for joy. So celebrate your life.

Barbara Johnson

Our sense of joy, satisfaction, and fulfillment in life increases, no matter what the circumstances, if we are in the center of God's will.

Billy Graham

Above and Beyond Our Worries

So don't worry about tomorrow, because tomorrow will have its own worries. Each day has enough trouble of its own.

—Matthew 6:34 NCV

When we're worried, there are two places we should take our concerns: to the people who love us and to God.

When troubles arise, it helps to talk about them with parents, grandparents, concerned adults, and trusted friends. But we shouldn't stop there: we should also talk to God through our prayers.

If you're worried about something, pray about it. Remember that God is always listening, and He always wants to hear from you.

So when you're upset about something, try this simple plan: talk and pray. Talk openly to the people who love you, and pray to the Heavenly Father who made you. The more you talk and the more you pray, the better you'll feel.

Worry does not empty tomorrow of its sorrow; it empties today of its strength.

Corrie ten Boom

Spending Time with God

Careful planning puts you ahead in the long run; hurry and scurry puts you further behind.

—Proverbs 21:5 MSG

How much time do you spend getting to know God? A lot? A little? Almost none? Hopefully, you answered, "a lot."

God loved this world so much that He sent His Son to save it. And now only one real question remains for you: what will you do in response to God's love? God deserves your prayers, your obedience, and your love—and He deserves these things all day every day, not just on Sunday mornings.

Slowly and surely, we learn the great secret of life, which is to know God.

Oswald Chambers

Frustration is not the will of God. There is time to do anything and everything that God wants us to do.

Elisabeth Elliot

The Best Excuse Is No Excuse

Each of us will be rewarded for his own hard work.

—1 Corinthians 3:8 TLB

Anybody can make up excuses, and you can too. But you shouldn't get into the habit of making too many excuses. Why? Because excuses don't work. And why don't they work? Because people have already heard so many excuses that most folks can recognize a phony excuse when they hear them.

So the next time you're tempted to make up an excuse, don't. Instead of making an excuse, do what you think is right. After all, the very best excuse of all . . . is no excuse.

Making up a string of excuses is usually harder than doing the work.

Marie T. Freeman

Replace your excuses with fresh determination.

Charles Swindoll

If You're Trying to Be Perfect

The Lord says, "Forget what happened before, and do not think about the past. Look at the new thing I am going to do. It is already happening. Don't you see it? I will make a road in the desert and rivers in the dry land."

—Isaiah 43:18-19 NCV

If you're trying to be perfect, you're trying to do something that's impossible. No matter how much you try, you can't be a perfect person . . . and that's okay.

God doesn't expect you to live a mistake-free life—and neither should you. In the game of life, God expects you to try, but He doesn't always expect you to win. Sometimes, you'll make mistakes, but even then, you shouldn't give up!

So remember this: you don't have to be perfect to be a wonderful person. In fact, you don't even need to be "almost-perfect." You simply must try your best and leave the rest up to God.

God is so inconceivably good. He's not looking for perfection. He already saw it in Christ. He's looking for affection.

Beth Moore

Get Enough Rest

Are you tired? Worn out? Burned out on religion? Come to me. Get away with me and you'll recover your life. I'll show you how to take a real rest. Walk with me and work with me…watch how I do it. Learn the unforced rhythms of grace. I won't lay anything heavy or ill-fitting on you. Keep company with me and you'll learn to live freely and lightly.

—Matthew 11:28-30 MSG

Even the most inspired Christians can, from time to time, find themselves "running out of gas." If you currently fit that description, remember that God expects you to do your work, but He also intends for you to rest. When you fail to take time for sufficient rest, you do a disservice to yourself, to your family, and to your friends.

Is your energy running low? Is your spiritual tank near empty? Are your emotions frayed? If so, it's time to turn your thoughts and your prayers to God. And when you're finished, it's time to treat yourself to a heaping helping of "R&R," which stands for "Rest and Renewal."

Life is strenuous. See that your clock does not run down.

Mrs. Charles E. Cowman

A Life of Prayer

May the words of my mouth and the thoughts of my heart be pleasing to you, O Lord, my rock and my redeemer.

—Psalm 19:14 NLT

Is prayer an integral part of your daily life, or is it a hit-or-miss habit? Do you "pray without ceasing," or is your prayer life an afterthought? Do you regularly pray in the solitude of the early morning darkness, or do you bow your head only when others are watching?

The quality of your spiritual life will be in direct proportion to the quality of your prayer life. Today, instead of turning things over in your mind, turn them over to God in prayer. Instead of worrying about your next decision, ask God to lead the way. Don't limit your prayers to the dinner table or the bedside table. Pray constantly about things great and small. God is always listening; it's up to you to do the rest.

The Christian on his knees sees more than the philosopher on tiptoe.

D. L. Moody

God insists that we ask,
not because He needs
to know our situation,
but because we need
the spiritual discipline of asking.

—

Catherine Marshall

Putting Faith to the Test

Be not afraid, only believe.

—Mark 5:36 KJV

Life is a tapestry of good days and difficult days, with good days predominating. During the good days, we are tempted to take our blessings for granted (a temptation that we must resist with all our might). But, during life's difficult days, we discover precisely what we're made of. And more importantly, we discover what our faith is made of.

Has your faith been put to the test yet? If so, then you know that with God's help, you can endure life's darker days. But if you have not yet faced the inevitable trials and tragedies of life-here-on-earth, don't worry: you will. And when your faith is put to the test, rest assured that God is perfectly willing—and always ready—to give you strength for the struggle.

Faith is strengthened only when we ourselves exercise it.

Catherine Marshall

Sharing the Good News

Go therefore and make disciples of all the nations, baptizing them in the name of the Father and of the Son and of the Holy Spirit, teaching them to observe all things that I have commanded you; and lo, I am with you always, even to the end of the age.

—Matthew 28:19-20 NKJV

After His resurrection, Jesus addressed His disciples. As recorded in the 28th chapter of Matthew, Christ instructed His followers to share His message with the world. This "Great Commission" applies to Christians of every generation, including our own.

As believers, we are called to share the Good News of Jesus with our families, with our neighbors, and with the world. Christ commanded His disciples to become fishers of men. We must do likewise, and we must do so today. Tomorrow may indeed be too late.

For every believer, the task, or mission, is to lead people to the truth of Jesus Christ.

Charles Stanley

The Path

But grow in the special favor and knowledge of our Lord and Savior Jesus Christ. To him be all glory and honor, both now and forevermore. Amen.

—2 Peter 3:18 NLT

When will you be a "fully-grown" Christian? Hopefully never—or at least not until you arrive in heaven! As a believer living here on planet earth, you're never "fully grown"; you always have the potential to keep growing.

In those quiet moments when you open your heart to God, the One who made you keeps remaking you. He gives you direction, perspective, wisdom, and courage.

Would you like a time-tested formula for spiritual growth? Here it is: keep studying God's Word, keep obeying His commandments, keep praying (and listening for answers), and keep trying to live in the center of God's will. When you do, you'll never stay stuck for long. You will, instead, be a growing Christian . . . and that's precisely the kind of Christian God wants you to be.

As I have continued to grow in my Christian maturity, I have discovered that the Holy Spirit does not let me get by with anything.

Anne Graham Lotz

The Blame Game

People's own foolishness ruins their lives, but in their minds they blame the Lord.

—Proverbs 19:3 NCV

When something goes wrong, do you look for somebody to blame? And do you try to blame other people even if you're the one who made the mistake? Hopefully not!

It's silly to try to blame other people for your own mistakes, so don't do it.

If you've done something you're ashamed of, don't look for somebody to blame; look for a way to say, "I'm sorry, and I won't make that same mistake again." Then, do your best to repair the mistake . . . and move on.

The main thing is this: we should never blame anyone or anything for our defeats. No matter how evil their intentions may be, they are altogether unable to harm us until we begin to blame them and use them as excuses for our own unbelief.

A. W. Tozer

Happiness Is . . .

Happy are the people who live at your Temple . . . . Happy are those whose strength comes from you.

—Psalm 84:4-5 NKJV

Do you seek happiness, abundance, and contentment? If so, here are some things you should do: Love God and His Son; depend upon God for strength; try, to the best of your abilities, to follow God's will; and strive to obey His Holy Word. When you do these things, you'll discover that happiness goes hand-in-hand with righteousness. The happiest people are not those who rebel against God; the happiest people are those who love God and obey His commandments.

What does life have in store for you? A world full of possibilities (of course it's up to you to seize them), and God's promise of abundance (of course it's up to you to accept it). So, remember to celebrate the life that God has given you. Your Creator has blessed you beyond measure. Honor Him with your prayers, your words, your deeds, and your joy.

We act as though comfort and luxury were the chief requirements of life, when all we need to make us really happy is something to be enthusiastic about.

Catherine Marshall

Choices Pleasing to God

If you need wisdom—if you want to know what God wants you to do—ask him, and he will gladly tell you. He will not resent your asking.

—James 1:5 NLT

All of us make choices—lots of them. When we make choices that are pleasing to our Heavenly Father, we are blessed. When we make choices that cause us to walk in the footsteps of God's Son, we enjoy the abundance that Christ has promised to those who follow Him. But when we make choices that are displeasing to God, we sow seeds that have the potential to bring forth a bitter harvest.

Today, as you encounter the challenges of everyday living, you will make hundreds of choices. Choose wisely. Make your thoughts and your actions pleasing to God. And remember: every choice that is displeasing to Him is the wrong choice—no exceptions.

Forbidden fruits create many jams.

Anonymous

Prayer: More Is Better

Rejoice always, pray without ceasing, in everything give thanks; for this is the will of God in Christ Jesus for you.

—1 Thessalonians 5:16-18 NKJV

Genuine, heartfelt prayer changes things and it changes us. When we lift our hearts to our Father in heaven, we open ourselves to a never-ending source of divine wisdom and infinite love.

Do you have questions that you simply can't answer? Ask for the guidance of your Father in heaven. Whatever your need, no matter how great or small, pray about it. Instead of waiting for mealtimes or bedtimes, follow the instruction of your Savior: pray always and never lose heart. And remember: God is not just near; He is here, and He's ready to talk with you. Now!

Two wings are necessary to lift our souls toward God: prayer and praise. Prayer asks. Praise accepts the answer.

Mrs. Charles E. Cowman

When the Path Is Dark

Though I sit in darkness, the Lord will be my light.
—Micah 7:8 Holman CSB

Doubts come in several shapes and sizes: doubts about God, doubts about the future, and doubts about our own abilities, for starters. But when doubts creep in, as they will from time to time, we need not despair.

God never leaves our side, not for an instant. He is always with us, always willing to calm the storms of life. When we sincerely seek His presence—and when we genuinely seek to establish a deeper, more meaningful relationship with Him—God is prepared to touch our hearts, to calm our fears, to answer our doubts, and to restore our confidence.

Ignoring Him by neglecting prayer and Bible reading will cause you to doubt.

Anne Graham Lotz

We are most vulnerable to the piercing winds of doubt when we distance ourselves from the mission and fellowship to which Christ has called us.

Joni Eareckson Tada

Trusting Your Conscience

Don't let evil get the best of you; get the best of evil by doing good.

—Romans 12:21 MSG

Billy Graham correctly observed, "Most of us follow our conscience as we follow a wheelbarrow. We push it in front of us in the direction we want to go." To do so, of course, is a profound mistake. Yet all of us, on occasion, have failed to listen to the voice that God planted in our hearts, and all of us have suffered the consequences.

God gave you a conscience for a very good reason: to make your path conform to His will. Wise believers make it a practice to listen carefully to that quiet internal voice. Count yourself among that number. When your conscience speaks, listen and learn. In all likelihood, God is trying to get His message through. And in all likelihood, it is a message that you desperately need to hear.

Guilt is a healthy regret for telling God one thing and doing another.

Max Lucado

When Things Go Wrong

I do not consider myself yet to have taken hold of it. But one thing I do: Forgetting what is behind and straining toward what is ahead, I press on toward the goal to win the prize for which God has called me heavenward in Christ Jesus.

—Philippians 3:13-14 NIV

When things don't turn out right, it's easy for most of us to give up. But usually, it's wrong. Why are we tempted to give up so quickly? Perhaps it's because we're afraid that we might embarrass ourselves if we tried hard but didn't succeed.

Here's something to remember: if you're having a little trouble getting something done, don't get mad, don't get frustrated, don't get discouraged, and don't give up. Just keep trying . . . and keep believing in yourself.

When you try hard—and keep trying hard—you can do amazing things . . . but if you quit at the first sign of trouble, you'll miss out. So here's a good rule to follow: when you have something that you want to finish, be brave enough (and wise enough) to finish it . . . you'll feel better about yourself when you do.

Failure is one of life's most powerful teachers. How we handle our failures determines whether we're going to simply "get by" in life or "press on."

Beth Moore

Obey God and Be Happy

I will praise you, Lord, with all my heart. I will tell all the miracles you have done. I will be happy because of you; God Most High, I will sing praises to your name.

—Psalm 9:1-2 NCV

Do you want to be happy? Here are some things you should do: Love God and His Son, Jesus; obey the Golden Rule; and always try to do the right thing. When you do these things, you'll discover that happiness goes hand-in-hand with good behavior.

The happiest people do not behave badly; the happiest people are not cruel or greedy. The happiest people don't say unkind things. The happiest people are those who love God and follow His rules—starting, of course, with the Golden one.

Those who are God's without reserve are, in every sense, content.

Hannah Whitall Smith

When we bring sunshine into the lives of others, we're warmed by it ourselves. When we spill a little happiness, it splashes on us.

Barbara Johnson

He Is Here

Every morning he wakes me. He teaches me to listen like a student. The Lord God helps me learn…

—Isaiah 50:4-5 NCV

Do you ever wonder if God is really here? If so, you're not the first person to think such thoughts. In fact, some of the biggest heroes in the Bible had their doubts—and so, perhaps, will you. But when questions arise and doubts begin to creep into your mind, remember this: God hasn't gone on vacation; He hasn't left town; and He doesn't have an unlisted number. You can talk with Him any time you feel like it. In fact, He's right here, right now, listening to your thoughts and prayers, watching over your every move.

Sometimes, you will allow yourself to become very busy, and that's when you may be tempted to ignore God. But, when you quiet yourself long enough to acknowledge His presence, God will touch your heart and restore your spirits. By the way, He's ready to talk right now. Are you?

God makes prayer as easy as possible for us. He's completely approachable and available, and He'll never mock or upbraid us for bringing our needs before Him.

Shirley Dobson

Living on Purpose

God chose you to be his people, so I urge you now to live the life to which God called you.

—Ephesians 4:1 NCV

Life is best lived on purpose. And purpose, like every-thing else in the universe, begins with God. Whether you realize it or not, God has a plan for your life, a direction in which He is leading you. When you welcome God into your heart and establish a genuine relationship with Him, He will begin, in time, to make His purposes known.

Sometimes, God's intentions will be clear to you; other times, God's plan will seem uncertain at best. But even on those difficult days when you are unsure which way to turn, you must never lose sight of these overriding facts: God created you for a reason; He has important work for you to do; and He's waiting patiently for you to do it.

And the next step is up to you.

God never calls without enabling us. In other words, if he calls you to do something, he makes it possible for you to do it.

Luci Swindoll

Helping the Helpless

In every way I've shown you that by laboring like this, it is necessary to help the weak and to keep in mind the words of the Lord Jesus, for He said, "It is more blessed to give than to receive."

—Acts 20:35 Holman CSB

The words of Jesus are clear: "Freely you have received, freely give" (Matthew 10:8 NIV). As followers of Christ, we are commanded to be generous with our friends, with our families, and especially with those in need. We must give freely of our time, our possessions, and our love.

In 2 Corinthians 9, Paul reminds us "God loves a cheerful giver" (v. 7 NKJV). So take God's words to heart and make this pledge: Be a cheerful, generous, courageous giver. The world needs your help, and you need the spiritual rewards that will be yours when you do.

It is the duty of every Christian to be Christ to his neighbor.

Martin Luther

God Will Forgive You

If we claim that we're free of sin, we're only fooling ourselves. A claim like that is errant nonsense. On the other hand, if we admit our sins—make a clean breast of them—he won't let us down; he'll be true to himself. He'll forgive our sins and purge us of all wrongdoing.

—1 John 1:8-9 MSG

Are you perfect? Of course not! Even if you're a very good person, you're bound to mistakes and lots of them.

When you make a mistake, you must try your best to learn from it (so that you won't make the very same mistake again). And, if you have hurt someone—or if you have disobeyed God—you must ask for forgiveness. And here's the good news: when you ask for God's forgiveness, He will always give it. God forgives you every single time you ask Him to. So ask!

Ask Christ to come into your heart to forgive you and help you. When you do, Christ will take up residence in your life by His Holy Spirit, and when you face temptations and trials, you will no longer face them alone.

Billy Graham

Small Acts of Kindness

Whatever you did for one of the least of these brothers of Mine, you did for Me

—Matthew 25:40 Holman CSB

Kindness is a choice. Sometimes, when we feel happy or generous, we find it easy to be kind. Other times, when we are discouraged or tired, we can scarcely summon the energy to utter a single kind word. But, God's commandment is clear: He intends that we make the conscious choice to treat others with kindness and respect, no matter our circumstances, no matter our emotions.

In the busyness and confusion of daily life, it is easy to lose focus, and it is easy to become frustrated. We are imperfect human beings struggling to manage our lives as best we can, but we often fall short. When we are distracted or disappointed, we may neglect to share a kind word or a kind deed. This oversight hurts others, but it hurts us most of all.

Today, slow yourself down and be alert for people who need your smile, your kind words, or your helping hand. Make kindness a centerpiece of your dealings with others. They will be blessed, and you will be, too.

First Things First

Happy is the person who finds wisdom, the one who gets understanding.

—Proverbs 3:13 NCV

When something important needs to be done, the best time to do it is sooner rather than later. But sometimes, instead of doing the smart thing (which, by the way, is choosing "sooner"), we may choose "later." When we do, we may pay a heavy price for our shortsightedness.

Are you one of those people who puts things off till the last minute? If so, it's time to change your ways. Your procrastination is probably the result of your shortsighted attempt to postpone (or avoid altogether) the discomfort that you associate with a particular activity. Get over it!

Whatever "it" is, do it now. When you do, you won't have to worry about "it" later.

A disciple is a follower of Christ. That means you take on His priorities as your own. His agenda becomes your agenda. His mission becomes your mission.

Charles Stanley

Miracles Great and Small

For nothing will be impossible with God.

—Luke 1:37 Holman CSB

God is a miracle worker. Throughout history He has intervened in the course of human events in ways that cannot be explained by science or human rationale. And He's still doing so today.

God's miracles are not limited to special occasions, nor are they witnessed by a select few. God is crafting His wonders all around us: the miracle of the birth of a new baby; the miracle of a world renewing itself with every sunrise; the miracle of lives transformed by God's love and grace. Each day, God's handiwork is evident for all to see and experience.

Today, seize the opportunity to inspect God's hand at work. His miracles come in a variety of shapes and sizes, so keep your eyes and your heart open. Be watchful, and you'll soon be amazed.

Are you looking for a miracle? If you keep your eyes wide open and trust in God, you won't have to look very far.

Marie T. Freeman

A Change of Heart

The one who conceals his sins will not prosper, but whoever confesses and renounces them will find mercy.

—Proverbs 28:13 Holman CSB

Who among us has sinned? All of us. But, God calls upon us to turn away from sin by following His commandments. And the good news is this: When we do ask God's forgiveness and turn our hearts to Him, He forgives us absolutely and completely.

Genuine repentance requires more than simply offering God apologies for the things we've done wrong. Real repentance may start with apologies to God, but it ends only when we turn away from the sins that distance us from Him. In truth, we offer our most meaningful apologies to God, not with our words, but with our actions. As long as we are still engaged in sin, we may be "repenting," but we have not fully "repented."

When true repentance comes, God will not hesitate for a moment to forgive, cast the sins in the sea of forgetfulness, and put the child on the road to restoration.

Beth Moore

Sharing with Your Family

A person who gives to others will get richer. Whoever helps others will himself be helped.

—Proverbs 11:25 ICB

A good place to start sharing is at home—but it isn't always an easy place to start. Sometimes, especially when we're tired or mad, we don't treat our family members as nicely as we should. And that's too bad!

Do you have brothers and sisters? Or cousins? If so, you're lucky.

Sharing your things—without whining or complaining—is a wonderful way to show your family that you love them. So the next time a brother or sister or cousin asks to borrow something, say "yes" without getting mad (or feeling resentful). It's a great way to say, "I love you."

In serving we uncover the greatest fulfillment within and become a stellar example of a woman who knows and loves Jesus.

Vonette Bright

God shows unbridled delight
when He sees people acting
in ways that honor Him:
when He receives worship,
when He sees faith demonstrated
in the most trying of
circumstances, and when He sees
tender love shared among
His people.

—

Bill Hybels

God Is Love

We know how much God loves us, and we have put our trust in him. God is love, and all who live in love live in God, and God lives in them.

—1 John 4:16 NLT

St. Augustine observed, "God loves each of us as if there were only one of us." Do you believe those words? Do you seek to have an intimate, one-on-one relationship with your Heavenly Father, or are you satisfied to keep Him at a "safe" distance?

Sometimes, in the crush of our daily duties, God may seem far away, but He is not. God is everywhere we have ever been and everywhere we will ever go. He is with us night and day; He knows our thoughts and our prayers. And, when we earnestly seek Him, we will find Him because He is here, waiting patiently for us to reach out to Him.

Let us reach out to Him today and always. And let us praise Him for the glorious gifts that have transformed us today and forever. Amen.

ssence of God's being is love—He never separates
f from that.

Kay Arthur